READINGS IN
LIBRARY
HISTORY

READINGS IN
LIBRARY
HISTORY

LESLIE W. DUNLAP

R. R. BOWKER CO.   New York & London 1972

Published by R. R. Bowker Co. (a Xerox company)
1180 Avenue of the Americas, New York, N.Y. 10036
Copyright © 1972 by Xerox Corporation
All rights reserved.
International Standard Book Number: 0–8352–0518–5
Library of Congress Catalog Card Number: 71–38429
Printed and bound in the United States of America

Books are not men,
and yet they are alive.
They are man's memory and his aspiration,
The link between his present and past,
The tools he builds with. . . .

Stephen Vincent Benet

Contents

List of Illustrations

Preface

The rise and fall of notable libraries during the ancient and middle ages receives scant attention in the literature of the civilizations which flourished from the seventh century B.C. until the sixteenth century A.D., and the facts and legends about these libraries have not been treated in an orderly fashion in the library histories available in English. Countless articles and books contain information about the libraries at Alexandria, Bobbio, Oxford, and elsewhere, but the reader who tries to find his way through this maze of bibliographic material is likely to become weary and confused.

For two decades, in my capacity as a university librarian and occasional instructor in library schools, I have read in the broad field of library history, and about ten years ago I decided to bring together the essays which best illuminate important segments of that subject. I wanted to present, in one easily-accessible volume, authoritative discussions of the libraries maintained by the Assyrians, Pharaohs, Byzantines, Muslims, Church Fathers, Carolingians, and others who formed and supported important collections of manuscript books for use and pleasure. In instances where no sketch of a library (Nineveh and Alexandria) or of the libraries in an era (the Roman) presented the salient facts in appropriate context, I undertook to tell the story anew. The book in hand contains the gleanings of innumerable hours of browsing and reading in hundreds, and possibly thousands of volumes, and presents to the reader a coherent narrative which contains discussions of notable ancient and medieval libraries.

Although this book was compiled primarily to help students in library schools who encounter difficulty in comprehending the development of libraries in early western civilizations, its contents should prove of interest to the reader who enjoys history in general. It can also be of use to the expert who is familiar with the sources for intensive study of a specific place and time, such as Northumbria in the eighth century, but may not know of the existence of the clay tablets once lodged in the palace of the Sargonides at Nineveh or of Petrarch's travels from Avignon, in search of the lost books of writers esteemed in ancient Greece and Rome.

My examination of the publications consulted in the preparation of this volume depended principally on the extensive collections of the libraries at the University of Iowa, in which I have worked since 1958. Since even rich collections cannot contain all publications of interest on most topics, books and copies of articles in periodicals housed in other libraries were borrowed for my use in Iowa City. I am especially indebted to Mrs. Julia Bartling and to Miss Ada Stoflet of the Reference Department of the University of Iowa Libraries for help in clarifying disputed points in the story, and for valued assistance in the selection of illustrations and in the preparation of a useful index. The typewriting of scores of pages of excerpts and of several versions of my manuscript was accomplished graciously, in the midst of regular duties, by Miss Doris Stuck, my secretary at the University of Iowa.

I would also like to express my appreciation to the members of my family for their patience and cooperation during the time I was writing and compiling this book.

List of Readings

The following is a bibliography of the sources from which the extracted readings have been drawn.

ALLEN, ROLAND. "Gerbert, Pope Silvester II." *The English Historical Review*, October 1892, pp. 626–635.

AMMIANUS, MARCELLINUS. *History*. Translated by John C. Rolfe. Vol. 1. Cambridge: Harvard University Press, 1935.

BURCKHARDT, JACOB. *The Civilisation of the Renaissance in Italy*. London: Sonnenschein, 1904.

DAWSON, CHRISTOPHER. *Medieval Essays*. London: Sheed and Ward, 1953.

DEBURY, RICHARD. *The Love of Books: The Philobiblon*, translated by E. C. Thomas. London: Alexander Moring, 1903.

DUCKETT, ELEANOR SHIPLEY. *Carolingian Portraits: A Study in the Ninth Century*. Ann Arbor: University of Michigan Press, 1962.

DUNLAP, LESLIE W. "Alexandria, the Capital of Memory." Lecture. Emporia, Kans.: Kansas State Teachers College of Emporia, March 1963.

DUNLAP, LESLIE W. "The Library at Nineveh." *Stechert-Hafner Book News*, March 1961, pp. 81–83.

DUNLAP, LESLIE W. "Under the Emperors." Unpublished essay.

ELTON, CHARLES AND ELTON, MARY. *The Great Book-Collectors*. London: Kegan Paul, 1893.

HARRISON, FREDERIC. *Byzantine History in the Early Middle Ages*. London: Macmillan, 1900.

HODGKIN, THOMAS. Introduction to *The Letters of Cassiodorus*. London: Henry Frowde, 1886.

KNOWLES, DOM M. D. "The Preservation of the Classics." In *The English Library before 1700*, by Francis Wormald and C. E. Wright. London: University of London, 1958.

MOORHOUSE, A. C. *Writing and the Alphabet*. London: Cobbett Press, 1946.

PADOVER, S. K. "Muslim Libraries." In *The Medieval Library*, by James Westfall Thompson. Chicago: University of Chicago Press, 1939.

RAND, EDWARD K. *Founders of the Middle Ages*. 2nd ed. Cambridge: Harvard University Press, 1941.

ST. BASIL. *The Letters of St. Basil*. Translated by R. J. Deferrari and Martin McGuire. Vol. 4. Cambridge: Harvard University Press, 1934.

ST. JEROME. *Select Letters of St. Jerome*. Translated by F. A. Wright. London: Heinemann, 1933.

SAVAGE, ERNEST A. *Old English Libraries*. London: Methuen, 1911.

SCHÜTZ, GÉZA. "Bibliotheca Corvina." *The Library Quarterly* 4 (1934): 552–563.

SCUDAMORE, WILLIAM E. "Libraries." In *A Dictionary of Christian Antiquities*, edited by William Smith and Samuel Cheetham, vol. 1. Hartford, Conn.: J. B. Burr, 1880.

SHEPHERD, WILLIAM. *The Life of Poggio Bracciolini*. London: T. Cadell, 1802.

STARR, CHESTER G. *Civilization and the Caesars*. Ithaca: Cornell University Press, 1954.

THURSTON, HERBERT. "Libraries." *The Catholic Encyclopedia* IX (1910): 230–231.

TILLEY, ARTHUR. *The Literature of the French Renaissance*. Vol. 1. Cambridge: University Press, 1904.

VICKERS, KENNETH H. *Humphrey, Duke of Gloucester*. London: Constable, 1907.

READINGS IN
LIBRARY
HISTORY

The Ancient World

Ancient civilization rose in the Fertile Crescent, a rainbow-like arc which begins at the west in the valley of the Nile, rises along the eastern shore of the Mediterranean through Jerusalem, Phoenicia, and Lebanon, reaches its zenith in the mountains which divide Turkey from Syria, and descends to the south and east between the Tigris and Euphrates rivers which flow into the Persian Gulf. About five hundred years before Christ, the center of civilization shifted westward, where it flourished for a thousand years on the shores of the Mediterranean Sea. Each city or state in the ancient world rose out of barbarism, struggled against the prospect of domination by would-be conquerors, was absorbed by other civilizations, and finally was engulfed by the hordes of barbarians who swarmed across the frontiers of the ancient civilizations clustered beside the Nile, between the Tigris and Euphrates rivers, and close by the waters of the great sea which washes the shores of Europe, Africa, and Asia Minor.

The wars and upheavals which rent and destroyed the ancient world also dispersed and consumed its books and libraries, and our knowledge of them depends on factors such as accidents of survival and discovery and on careful and sympathetic study. An ancient library, Aristotle's, for example, is frequently mentioned in histories, but details are few and we know nothing about the titles of his books or

1

their ultimate fate. The cynical remark, "History may not repeat itself, but historians do," is especially applicable to works on the ancient world; thus, writer after writer refers to Marc Antony's magnificent gift of the library at Pergamum to his fascinating Queen of Egypt, yet we do not know whether Cleopatra received the books. Not one of the libraries of the ancient world escaped ruin, and our knowledge of their existence must be pieced together from scattered and sometimes conflicting bits of information.

INTRODUCTION OF WRITING

Written records have been accumulated and stored since the early Sumerians discovered the art of writing, about five thousand years ago, and archaeologists have unearthed tens of thousands of tablets among the ruins of Sumerian temples in ancient Mesopotamia. The Sumerians were a short, stocky people with high, straight noses, receding foreheads, and a common language and religion, who lived in the third millennium before Christ in cities between the Tigris and Euphrates rivers. In each of the Sumerian cities a great temple was erected in honor of the locally favored deity, and here were performed fertility rites and human sacrifices similar to those found among the Aztecs and other early civilizations. Financial support for the temple and its priesthood came from land worked by tenants under long-term contracts which had to be intelligible to persons other than the participants. This need led to the development of conventional symbols which would be widely understood, and the Sumerians inaugurated schools for the scribes who had to draft commercial documents. Writing was used first "not for magical and liturgical purposes but for practical business and administration."[1] As knowledge increased among the Sumerian priests and scribes, additional information was written down in the complicated script which was understood only by the initiated who had memorized a thousand cuneiform characters. The temple libraries in Sumeria, three thousand years before Christ, contained commercial accounts, grammatical exercises for young scribes, mathematical texts, treatises on medicine and astrology, and collections of hymns, prayers, and incantations. Here too were the

[1] V. Gordon Childe, *Man Makes Himself* (New York: New American Library, 1951), p. 148.

beginnings of literature—four thousand years later we hearken to the plaint of the Sumerian singer who had been driven from his city by the conquerors from East and West:

> Birdlike from my shrine he chased me,
> From my city like a bird he chased me, me sighing,
> "Far behind, behind me is my temple."[2]

The written records made by the Sumerians and their successors in Mesopotamia, the Babylonians and the Assyrians, have survived in such numbers because the scribes of the three civilizations wrote on clay. This material, common in the fertile plain between the Tigris and Euphrates rivers where trees and stone are scarce, was carefully kneaded and formed into cylinders or tablets which were impressed while wet. The rapidity with which the clay dried necessitated quick and accurate writing, and a wedge-shaped stylus (hence "cuneiform") was used to mark the wet surface. A contract written on wet clay could be stamped with the seals of the parties involved, and the agreement could be made practically indestructible through baking by fire. The finished documents could be stored on shelves or in baskets which could be labeled for easy reference. Clay is bulkier and heavier than is desirable for frequent exchanges between distant points, but its obvious merits made clay the principal writing material during the twenty-five hundred years that civilization flourished in ancient Mesopotamia.

The contribution which the invention of writing made to the development of civilization in Mesopotamia is summarized in the chapter, "The Historical Influence of Writing," in A. C. Moorhouse's Writing and the Alphabet (London: Cobbett Press, 1946), pp. 68–74. Of special interest to the historian of libraries is the impulse which led the Sumerians to commit to writing their legends and lore at the time their political power was passing to the Babylonians (see the last paragraph in the following excerpt, which is reprinted here with the permission of the present holder of the copyright).

In the ancient tradition of the Chinese, the Egyptians and the Babylonians, the invention of writing was made by divine beings.

[2] As quoted in Will Durant, Our Oriental Heritage (New York: Simon and Schuster, 1935), p. 123.

It is natural that such a remarkable possession of man should have been regarded as something beyond his unaided powers of creation, and especially so at a time when the gradual development of writing from its early pictorial form was not understood. But there is another reason for putting a high value upon the art of writing, though it is one which could hardly have been properly appreciated by the makers of the fables. It is, that writing is pre-eminently the art of civilisation. Indeed, it has made our civilisation possible—not only by permitting the existence of a highly developed literature and science, but by playing a vital part in the reorganisation of society which produced the complex states of ancient and modern times. Both public and private life are profoundly changed by its acquisition. Without it we could not have risen far from a condition of barbarism.

In considering the effects of the introduction of writing, it will be convenient to look first at the area of the Rivers Tigris and Euphrates where cuneiform arose. Our knowledge of conditions here is particularly rich, and they may be taken as a general indication of how the use of writing developed in the ancient world.

The fact that at once strikes our attention is the close association of writing with the temples. The earliest written tablets are found in Sumerian temple ruins, and temple finds always provide some of the richest stores for the archaeologists. The explanation is that the religious communities were the most important in the contemporary society. They formed permanent colleges, whose members changed, but which remained corporately the same. Inevitably this led to an accumulation of power in their hands. The estates that formed the temple property (being nominally the possession of the god), made them wealthy. The priests managed their estates, letting them out for rent; or else they farmed them themselves, and for this purpose had to employ labour. There was industrial activity supervised from the temple, and often actually carried out on its premises. For example, for Lagash, a small Sumerian city, we have the records of the temple of Baü. It employed bakers (forty-eight, including twenty-seven slaves), brewers (thirty-one), spinners and weavers, a smith and other artisans. Another outlet for the wealth of the temple was to lend it at interest, which we know that the Babylonians did.

Activities of this sort required writing. It is thus only natural that the oldest specimens of Sumerian ideography relate to temple accounts. Unless they kept records, the priests would not know how much their revenue was, who had and who had not paid them the produce due on their estates, nor even whether some member of the priesthood was wrongly appropriating for his own use some of the temple's wealth.

Very large numbers of clay tablets have been discovered which were used in the temple counting-houses. There was in this connection one special difficulty to be overcome, which helps to account for the number of the remains. A clay tablet does not remain damp for long, and has to be written on before it dries. The temple clerks therefore wrote a separate temporary memorandum in the first place to record each item of receipt, and waited until a number of these had been collected. Then from this material a weekly ledger account was prepared, followed by monthly ones, and finally the whole year's account. The number of the temporary memoranda used in a year would run into thousands.

The temples had to provide schools in order to ensure the continuance of writing—and especially, at the start, to see that the same conventions were followed in the choice of suitable signs. In this way they prevented the anarchy that would have arisen from the existence of numerous alternative ideograms. We possess specimens of tablets similar to our copy-books, which the pupils used in the schools. On one side of them are signs made by the teacher, and on the other the pupil's imitation of them. As the writing developed and became more perfect, it was used to record religious texts, hymns and descriptions of ceremonial, and the scientific knowledge of the day in the form of divination and astronomy. A collection of literary and scientific works slowly formed itself in the temples, which became more and more the centre of learning. The standard works were used in the schools to provide material for copying. This has led to the curious result that we have far more copies of the earlier parts of such

Plate I Cuneiform Clay Tablets

works than of the later, which are sometimes altogether wanting. For the pupils all began their copying with the early passages, and their interest was apt to flag before they had got through their task—if, indeed, they had ever meant to finish it.

Thus, writing served well for the purposes of a priest-directed society of a gradually increasing complexity. But it was not possible to confine the knowledge of it to the servants of the temple, greatly though it might have been to their interest to do so. Whether it was with willing co-operation or without it that the art of writing spread outside the temple walls, we do not know. What is plain is that the reins of temporal power began to pass out of priestly hands when their monopoly of writing disappeared.

In the empire of the Babylonians, and then, after them, of the Assyrians, writing was eventually used for practically all of the diverse purposes which it serves to-day.

Commercial use was still to the fore. Indeed, this type of use is quite characteristic of the Semitic civilisations of Mesopotamia, and may fairly be taken as a sign of one side of their special development. The relative frequency of occurrence of tablets of this sort is well marked when we contrast the remains of writing of other ancient civilisations, e.g., the Chinese, the Egyptian, or the Greek. Of course, in some degree the contrast is misleading. We are fortunate in possessing in very great abundance the day-to-day memoranda of the people of Babylonia and Assyria, on account of the fact that they were written on indestructible clay. Those who wrote them often did not intend that their notes should survive for more than a few days: but in fact they have lasted for thousands of years. On the other hand the ephemeral writing of other countries has generally been made on equally ephemeral materials (e.g., paper, wax, etc.). Nevertheless, when full account has been taken of this feature, we are justified in stating that cuneiform not only took its origin in a form of commercial use, but continued throughout its history to have special association with it.

In addition to the business accounts and ledgers of private firms, we have contracts drawn up in cuneiform. It was laid down by law that all business deals should be so documented, and the record was completed by the addition of the signatures of the contracting parties and of witnesses. But though the employment of writing was thus very widespread, the number of persons who could themselves write (and read) was small. Accordingly, a way had to be found for documents to be attested which did not require writing. Sometimes a witness impressed on the clay the mark of his finger. More often he used a seal of the type known to us as a cylinder seal, from its shape. The seal bore as a design a scene from daily life, or from sacred legend, and its impression on the document took the place of its owner's personal signature. The same procedure was adopted in drawing up the records of personal affairs, such as betrothals and wills.

One of the most remarkable pieces of evidence of Assyrian commercial enterprise is a series of tablets from Asia Minor, known as Cappadocian, and principally found by the ancient town of Caesarea. They date from about 2000 B.C., and represent the business correspondence of a colony of Assyrian merchants and commercial agents. These people were in regular touch both with agents in other parts of the country and with their homeland. It is notable that tablets of a literary nature are completely lacking.

To what other uses was cuneiform writing put by the civilisations of Mesopotamia? They can be briefly summed up under the headings literary, historical, administrative, legal and scientific.

The literature of Babylonia and Assyria was mainly religious, consisting of hymns and spells, and legends: there is, however, also evidence for epics with an historical basis. It was at a relatively late date that it was first committed to writing—the greater part of the early texts were written down shortly after 2000 B.C., probably in the reign of the great Babylonian king Hammurabi. Previously they were kept alive by oral tradition, in the same way as primitive literature in many other parts of the world: for example, the lengthy poems of Homer in Greece, the hymns of the Rig-Veda in India, and in more recent times the Border Ballads in Scotland. It is plain, therefore, that writing was not, either in Mesopotamia or elsewhere, necessary for the creation or continued existence of the prayers and songs with which the divine powers were to be moved, nor for the tales which glorified the famous deeds of the past. But there was a particular reason which probably led to the general commitment of literature to cuneiform writing in Babylonia, at the start of the second millennium B.C. At that time the Sumerians were finally giving up their political supremacy to the Semitic people of Babylon, and the non-Semitic Sumerian language was passing into oblivion so far as everyday use was concerned. But the ancient religious texts which had proved their use, according to current belief, over so many centuries, were Sumerian texts, and it was unthinkable that they should be abandoned. Who knew how much of their power derived from the exact form of words that was hallowed by tradition? Yet how was the ancient form to be preserved, when the language itself was becoming less familiar? The solution that was adopted was, to preserve the texts by writing them down, and Sumerian was enabled to remain the language of religion.

THE EARLIEST LIBRARIES

Assyria

The earliest libraries in which the Sumerians tried to preserve their culture from absorption in that of their Babylonian conquerors were formed early in the second millennium before Christ, but the Babylonians did not profit from the example until they in turn had given way to the Assyrians (1100 B.C.). In both instances the clay tablets made in desperation were stored with the archives of an established "temple library," and fell in the ruins when the temple was destroyed. The Assyrian kings were sufficiently interested in the earlier Mesopotamian cultures of Sumer and Babylon to collect and to transcribe their clay tablets. Moreover, the later Assyrian kings provided for the translation of the tablets in the older languages into the Assyrian vernacular. According to Edward Chiera in They Wrote on Clay, 2nd ed. (Chicago: University of Chicago Press, 1955), "The old Sumerian stories were published as they were found, with an interlinear translation in the Assyrian language" (p. 174).

The bilingual texts were stored in palace libraries, the best known of which is that of Ashurbanipal at Nineveh, "which fortunately [for modern scholarship] was found at the very beginning of Mesopotamian excavations" (p. 175).

The story of "The Library at Nineveh" is told briefly in my article in the Stechert-Hafner Book News, March 1961, pp. 81–83:

> According to the prophet Isaiah, the Lord God of Hosts raised up the King of Assyria to punish the nations which had worshiped idols and graven images:
>
> > And against the people of my wrath will I give him a charge,
> > To take the spoil, and to take the prey,
> > And to tread them down like the mire of the streets.
>
> The assignment fit the Assyrian like a glove and soon he could make the proud boast:
>
> > And my hand hath found as a nest
> > The riches of the people;
> > And as one gathereth eggs that are left,
> > Have I gathered all the earth;
> > And there was none that moved the wind,
> > Or opened the mouth or peeped.
>
> In the Book of Kings we read how Sennacherib, King of Assyria, moved with a great host against Jerusalem and how King Hezekiah in "a day of trouble" sought help from Isaiah. The prophet counseled Hezekiah to resist the Assyrians because the Lord God of Israel would suffer no longer the affronts of the haughty Assyrian and would send him back by the way he came. That very night the angel of the Lord smote more than five thousand Assyrians in their camp, "So Sennacherib King of Assyria departed, and went and returned, and dwelt at Nineveh." This was the seat of his palace and of the Royal Library of the Sargonides (722–626 B.C.), the earliest library worthy of the name.
>
> The Assyrians had dwelt in Mesopotamia since about 3000 B.C., when they built the city of Ashur on a promontory overlooking the Tigris. Their land to the north of their first capital, in contrast to the alluvial plain near the mouth of the Twin Rivers, was hilly, wooded, and contained stone. Lodged between

the Babylonians and Sumerians several hundred miles to the south and the barbarous mountain tribes even closer to the north, the Assyrians received blows on both sides; but, instead of weakening the new nation, the struggles strengthened its fibre. By the time of Ashurnasirpal (883–859 B.C.), the Assyrians had conquered Lebanon to the east and Armenia to the north, and their conqueror set about to develop his empire and to build a new capital at Nimrud. Each succeeding Assyrian king waged new campaigns, and the accession of Sargon II in 721 B.C. ushered in the day of Assyria's greatest glory (721–606 B.C.).

The thousands of clay tablets and the miles of sculptured reliefs discovered in the ruins of the palaces of Sargon and his dynasty (the Sargonides) provide us with "more of the trivial details of everyday family life" in the Late Assyrian period than we have for "the Norman peasant." The daily routine of the rank and file of the Assyrians in the seventh century before Christ was not very different from that of the inhabitants of Iraq before recent innovations in transportation and technology, but their rulers were a breed as distinctive as the colossal man-headed winged bulls which flanked their palace gates. "The Assyrian came down like the wolf on the fold," wrote the quotable Byron; and his characterization of the Assyrian as a "wolf" is remembered by every schoolboy who has learned "The Destruction of Sennacherib." Every war plumbs new depths of horror, but the mutilation of the vanquished seldom is treated with the simplicity and directness shown in Assyrian art. The Assyrians excelled in both war and brutality, and the terror they wrought among their enemies has bedimmed their major accomplishments in the construction of cities and palaces, in the artistic representations of their military exploits and peacetime diversions, and in the establishment of libraries.

The first library of consequence, the Royal Library founded and maintained at Nineveh by the Sargonides, was begun under Sargon II; additions were made by his son, Sennacherib, and by his son, Esarhaddon; but it was Sargon's great-grandson, Ashurbanipal (668–626 B.C.), who enlarged the collections into a storehouse of information about early civilizations in Mesopotamia. Ashurbanipal's role in the development of the Royal Library is certain, because practically every important tablet found at Nineveh bears this legend:

> Palace of Ashurbanipal, king of the world . . . who has possessed himself of a clear eye and the choice art of tablet-writing, such as none among the kings, my predecessors, had acquired. The wisdom of Nabu, the ruled line, all that there is, have I inscribed upon tablets, checking and revising it, and that I might see and read them, have I placed them within my palace.

Although Ashurbanipal boasted that he was the first of his line to read and write, iron was in his blood and in his weapons; and like the earlier Assyrian kings, he was a great hunter and a fierce warrior. According to his own count, Ashurbanipal killed 30 elephants, 257 wild animals from his chariot, and 370 lions with the spear; and his military campaigns extended to both ends of the Fertile Crescent. The Egyptians rebelled against Assyrian domination, and in retaliation Ashurbanipal carried from the temples at Thebes enormous loot, including gold, silver, statues, and sculptured obelisks. Ashurbanipal's Egyptian expedition consumed men and resources, and Elam at the other end of his empire chose this opportunity to defy his authority. The Assyrian's sack of Susa was complete; more than a month was spent in rapacity and then Ashurbanipal ordered salt to be scattered over the ruins and weeds to be sown. Ashurbanipal's own account of the pillage concludes:

> The voice of man, the steps of flocks and herds, the happy shouts of mirth I put an end to them in its field which I left for the asses, the gazelles and all manner of wild beasts to people.

Our earliest library began as an archival repository for letters received from administrators of distant parts of the Assyrian empire and for business contracts, and to these were added cuneiform historical tablets which dated from 1280 B.C. The archival and historical records could not be used effectively without access to works of reference such as sign lists, arithmetic tables, and religious texts, and these were acquired to meet specific needs. The third phase in the development of this library was reached when tablets were collected because they might sometime prove useful. The realization of the potential value of records to posterity was Ashurbanipal's contribution, and his thought is explicit in some of the colophons, "For the sake of dis[tant] days he collated [the tablet] [and] placed [it] in his palace." Mindful of their possible later use, Ashurbanipal directed Shadunu with assistance from three helpers and the learned men of Borsippa to obtain all of "the precious tablets which are known to you and are not in Assyria. . . . No one shall withhold tablets from you, and if you see any tablets and ritual texts about which I have not written to you, and they are suitable for my palace, select [them], collect them and send [them to me]."

More than two-thirds of the twenty-five thousand tablets found in the Royal Library at Nineveh contain texts made in response to Ashurbanipal's orders. "Almost every class of literary effort" was preserved, "the only kind wanting being the love-song, which certainly existed in Assyria." The Assyrians had learned the efficacy of some five hundred drugs in the treatment of the diseases and ailments that plague mankind, but their knowledge of medicine was overlain with religious beliefs and with predictions based on the movements of heavenly bodies. If we may judge from the tablets found at Nineveh, the life of an Assyrian was directed by astrological forecasts and by omens deduced from the most insignificant occurrences. To combat evil forces and to placate his pantheon of deities, the Assyrian employed incantations, prayers, and hymns. The Assyrian also had his legendary heroes, such as the great Gilgamesh (two-thirds god and one-third man), and the twelve tablets which relate his adventures contain the Babylonian account of the Deluge. The court at Nineveh also manifested a keen interest in languages, for Ashurbanipal ordered lists to be made of cuneiform characters in both Sumerian and Akkadian. When the Assyrian King directed copies of works in Sumerian to be made for his Library, he required the scribe to write the Assyrian translation for each line of the original. The care with which the translations and dictionaries were prepared for the instruction of Ashurbanipal's scribes has made this group of tablets invaluable to students of his and of earlier Mesopotamian civilizations.

Although the use of a collection that flourished seven centuries before Christ must be left largely to conjecture, two letters are extant that pertain to the consultation of materials in the Royal Library. In one, King Esarhaddon asked a palace official, perhaps the librarian, to furnish the phraseology from a particular tablet; for, as he wrote, "I wish to hear how it is written in a text." Presumably, complicated astronomical calculations could not have been made by Assyrian astrologists without frequent reference to mathematical tabulations in the Library, and the legal contracts in the collection must have been consulted by the parties thereto at least until the obligations were fulfilled. There are other definite indications that the tablets were used: first, a curse "terrible and merciless as long as he lives" was laid on whomever stole or defaced a tablet; and second, Ashurbanipal explained that he had developed the Library for his "royal contemplation and recital." Ashurbanipal might well have ordered the twelve tablets that contain the story of the legendary Gilgamesh, "He who hath seen the spring," to be fetched from the library rooms near the palace entrance and read before his court:

> He went on a long far way
> Giving himself trial and distress;
> Wrote then on a stone tablet the whole of his labor.

Nineveh fell in 606 B.C. to the Medes, and the tablets in the Library of the Sargonides were broken and scattered on the floor "to a height of a foot or more." When the palace of Sennacherib was discovered in the middle of the last century by Henry Layard, he at first believed the cuneiform fragments to be bits of pottery decorated in an unusual manner, and not until after he had returned to England did he learn the importance of strange markings on the clay tablets, which range in size from one inch by seven-eighths of an inch to fifteen by eight and five-eighths inches. Darius' great inscription in Babylonian, Persian, and Sumerian on the rock at Behistun had been deciphered shortly before by G. F. Grotefend and Sir Henry Rawlinson; and, after the tablets found at Nineveh had been shipped to London, Rawlinson undertook to translate the cuneiform writing in the Sumerian and Akkadian languages. With the publication of Rawlinson's translations in the 1860's, the science of Assyriology was born. Most of the clay fragments from the Royal Library at Nineveh now are in the treasured "Kouyunjik Collection" in the British Museum: Kouyunjik, "the little lamb," is the name of the mound that concealed for more than twenty-five centuries the tablets Ashurbanipal had placed in his palace library "for the sake of distant days."

Egypt

Although primacy in many cultural developments belongs to the ancient Egyptians, writing, as we have seen, developed first in Iraq. To be sure, Egypt early developed a series of picture signs, but the utilization of a particular Egyptian sign for a consonantal sound was a fifteenth century B.C. "innovation of a subject people, the Canaanites."[3] References to a "sacred library" in the great temple at Thebes are common because of a doorway inscription, "Healing-place of the Soul," copied in the first century after Christ by a Roman historian, yet nothing is known about the contents of such a room in the great mortuary temple built by Rameses II, who died in 1225 B.C. There also are references to medical and literary rolls preserved in ancient Egyptian temples, but these seem to have been records created by the priests and temple scribes (archives), rather than books collected for the use of others (libraries). The evidence is so scanty and indecisive that John A. Sperry, Jr. concluded in his "Egyptian Libraries: A Survey of the Evidence," Libri (1957), "a more complete and careful examination of archaeological and historical materials . . . is needed in order that more light may be thrown upon the subject" (p. 153). Sperry suggests "that the Alexandrian Library, too, may have had its antecedents in an older Egyptian institution" (p. 151), but the greatest library of the ancient world, although located at the mouth of the Nile, was of Greek origin.

---

[3] John A. Wilson, *The Burden of Egypt* (Chicago: University of Chicago Press, 1951), p. 191.

HELLENIC LIBRARIES

After a careful review of the development of literature and of a reading public in the early part of the fourth century B.C., Frederic G. Kenyon observes in Books and Readers in Ancient Greece and Rome (Oxford: Clarendon Press, 1932): "The history of libraries in the Greek and Graeco–Roman world is rightly taken to start with the foundation of the Museum at Alexandria; but the foundation of the Museum and of the great Alexandrian Library was made possible by the change of habit which took form in the time, and largely under the influence, of Aristotle" (p. 25). Kenyon continues: "The causes which operated in Egypt operated also in Syria and Asia Minor, and may be assumed to have produced similar results. . . . The main centres, notably Alexandria, but also Antioch, Pergamum, and the other great cities of the Near East, were the seats of libraries and the homes of scholars; and Greek literature was the natural heritage of the Greek-speaking population throughout the Hellenistic kingdoms" (pp. 36–37).

Very little is known about the libraries at Antioch and Pergamum, but there is enough in print to warrant reconstructing the story of the Alexandrian Library. Here is the version in my lecture, "Alexandria, the Capital of Memory," published by the Kansas State Teachers College of Emporia, March 1963, pp. 14–25:

> Although Alexandria is on the soil of Egypt, the city was known in ancient times as "Alexandria by Egypt" since the culture of its leaders was rooted deep in the mountains and isles of Greece. You will recall that the early Greeks had fought for centuries among themselves until in the seventh century before Christ two cities, Sparta and Athens, dominated the mountainous peninsula. The former, an aristocratic society, controlled the Southern Peloponnesus; and the latter, a comparatively democratic city, ruled Attica and, by the time of Pericles (5th century, B.C.), much of Greece. Sparta in 404 broke the Athenian sway and established an empire which fell in 362 to Thebes. The Theban confederacy soon gave way to the Athenian, and the manifest weaknesses of all the Greek cities made them vulnerable to the

warlike Macedonians led successively by Philip and by his son, Alexander the Great (336–323 B.C.).

During the interminable conflicts in the mountainous peninsula (and in part because of them) Greek emigrants founded new cities on all the coasts of the Mediterranean until Plato could observe, "Like frogs around a pond, we have settled down upon the shores of this sea." Although the ancient Greeks could not live in peace at home, the colonists shared a common culture which tied them to each other and to their homeland. In addition to feeling loyal attachments to their native cities, the colonists spoke the same musical language, thrilled to the same tales of legendary heroes told by Homer and by the Greek dramatists, competed in similar games and athletic contests, worshiped the same gods, and shared a common delight in the beauty of form achieved in sculpture and in architecture. The Greeks loved art and beauty, and they esteemed reason and used it to understand better their world and their lives. The Greek world was tied with strong bonds; indeed, "all civilized nations, in all that concerns the activity of the intellect, are colonies of Hellas."

Although the early Greeks loved literature, little reading was done in Greece before the fifth century B.C. Since the ninth century, the Homeric epics had been declaimed to enthralled audiences and lyrics were sung to musical accompaniment, but the poems were rarely put in writing. During the Golden Age of Greek literature, schools became common, and in Athens even women and slaves were permitted to learn to read and write. In Socrates' lifetime (469?–399 B.C.) the literary masterpieces were widely known, and this condition presupposes the availability of many copies. Socrates scoffed that the speeches of the orator Isocrates were sold by the bundle; and in *The Frogs*, Aristophanes gibes, "nobody lacked a book on the subject." Books were not confined to the Athenian capital, for Xenophon noted that books were part of the cargoes of ships wrecked on the shores of the Black Sea. Nevertheless, the Age of Pericles was not bookish: the tragedian Euripides owned one of the few notable libraries, and this circumstance evoked a sneer from Aristophanes, the wry writer of comedies. At the end of the fifth century, books were cheap and accessible in Athens, but reading still did not rate highly as a means of training the mind.

In the fourth century "the Greek world passed from oral instruction to the habit of reading," and the key figure in the transition is that of the great Aristotle (384–322 B.C.). Aristotle formed the most famous private library of the ancient world, and he used the books in the preparation of his scientific treatises. The scholar kept a record of his systematic reading, and his surveys of the opinions of predecessors reveal the range of his studies. . . . Aristotle's greatest contribution to the development of libraries probably was the instruction he gave for four years to the young and wild Alexander, heir to the throne of Macedonia. The influence of a teacher on a student ordinarily defies description; but, if Aristotle's Macedonian pupil had not become a Hellene, Greek civilization could not have flowered into Hellenism.

On the assassination of Philip (336), Alexander seized his father's throne and compelled the allegiance of the rebellious Greek states. Ambition and an empty treasury drove him two years later against the Persians, and at Issus in Asia Minor he defeated a large force under Darius III and the Persian Empire was at an end. Instead of pursuing the "Great King" and his demoralized army, Alexander wisely chose to bring under control the abandoned Persian possessions beside the eastern Mediterranean and thus to deprive the Persian fleet of its bases. Alexander was hailed in Syria as deliverer, and he marched in triumph southwest to the oasis of Siwa in Libya where he was received by the priest of Ammon as the son of God. On his return to the Delta of the Nile, Alexander decided to build a new capital for Egypt which would open onto the Greek world. The site of a poor fishing village on a narrow strip of land between Lake Mareotis and the sea was selected for the new city, and Alexander marked its boundaries, principal streets, and the locations of palaces and temples. The restless and brilliant Macedonian did not see his plans realized for he died at Babylon at age thirty-three, but the city named after him was destined to become "the most successful of all Alexander's foundations."

Asked on his deathbed to whom his empire should be left, Alexander replied, "To the strongest"; and five of his Macedonian chieftains proceeded to divide the spoils. Out of this division came the three great monarchies, Macedonia (Alexander's homeland), Seleucid (Asia Minor), and Egypt, which were to dominate the Hellenistic world until the triumph of Rome. The richest part of the Empire, Egypt, was allotted to Ptolemy, one of the Conqueror's seven bodyguards, who, instead of contesting for more land, devoted himself "to cultivating his garden."

Ptolemy, the son of Lagus, was a practical man who esteemed learning; and, after he had become master of Egypt, he proceeded to develop the country and to adorn its capital. For almost twenty years after the death of Alexander, Ptolemy governed Egypt as a province of the Macedonian Empire, but in 304 B.C. he assumed the titles of King and Soter (Savior) and established the dynasty which ruled Egypt until the voluptuous Cleopatra was conquered by Romans in 30 B.C. Although not a visionary, Ptolemy Soter took three steps which made Alexandria the intellectual and spiritual center of Hellenism. Firstly, Ptolemy enshrined the body of Alexander in a mausoleum which was visited for more than three centuries by the curious and the contemplative. Secondly, Alexander had dreamed of a union of Europe and Asia, and the first Ptolemy fostered the cult of Serapis which blended Greek and Egyptian (Oriental) religious elements. Finally, Ptolemy Soter founded the Alexandrian Museum and Library as proposed by a refugee from Athens, Demetrius of Phaleron.

To develop his kingdom, Ptolemy encouraged Macedonians and Greeks with special skills and learning to emigrate to Alexandria, and among the intellectuals who responded were the mathematician Euclid, the poet Callimachus, and the accomplished statesman Demetrius. Demetrius was born about 350 B.C. in Phaleron (Athens' seaport) of humble parents, but he received the liberal education provided upper-class Athenian youths. As a student in the Lyceum under Theophrastus, the principal disciple of Aristotle, Demetrius observed the importance of a library for reference and for study. While in his twenties, Demetrius entered public life, and he rose to become viceroy of Athens. The new governor administered the city with considerable success, but he adorned his person and indulged his appetites for pleasure and delicacies like an Oriental prince. In the midst of his administrative duties and decadent delights, Demetrius, in the best Athenian tradition, pursued scholarship and letters. "He was the last figure of the great Attic period of letters, or shall we say the first of the Alexandrian age."

After the fall of Athens in 307 b.c., Demetrius was banished, and ten years passed before he reached Alexandria where he promptly became an advisor to Ptolemy I. According to most students, Demetrius induced the King of Egypt to establish in his capital an academy similar to the Athenian Museum where he had studied under Theophrastus. In the new institution scholars supported at public expense would devote their time and energies to science and literature. Those admitted lived in cloisters adjoining the temple of the Muses, and they disputed moot points in nearby alcoves and lecture halls. Although the Museum scholars were free to do as they pleased, the money for their support came from the royal purse and this understandably affected their work. The poets and scientists of the Museum avoided offense to the Royal Family, and to gratify the Palace the intellectuals produced victory odes, marriage hymns, funeral dirges, mechanical toys, maps, and engines of war. This direct dependence of the Museum on the Palace made sycophants of the scholars until the bitter Timon characterized them as "fatted fowls in a coop." The Museum typified the derivative culture of Alexandria: significant original creations were rare indeed, but here the laurels of Greek civilization were kept green for seven centuries. From first to last, the Greek intellectuals in Alexandria found nurture in the Museum's Library.

Classical scholars who attribute the foundation of the Alexandrian Museum to the influence of Demetrius usually identify him as the moving spirit behind the formation of the Museum's Library. While a student at the Lyceum in Athens, Demetrius had had access to Aristotle's library; and, if he did lay the plans for the Alexandrian Museum, he would have known the need of the scholars in Alexandria for a first-class library. Poets and scientists from established cities all over the Greek world would have been unable and unwilling to pursue learning in the raw capital beside the Delta of the Nile without a collection of the records of the Hellenistic and other civilizations. Details of any arrangements between Ptolemy and Demetrius for the establishment of the Museum and Library are unknown, but the Museum soon acquired large quantities of manuscripts presumably recommended by Demetrius. The Alexandrian Library burgeoned; and, at the end of the Soter's reign, the collection numbered about 200,000 volumes. When the King questioned Demetrius about future growth of the Library, the refugee from Athens "flattered himself with the hope of having 500,000 in his charge."

After the death of Ptolemy Soter (283 B.C.), Demetrius was banished from Alexandria by Ptolemy II for having supported the unsuccessful aspirant to the crown; but the Library he had founded continued to grow apace. According to the best sources, the collection contained at the end of the third century B.C. about 400,000 rolls, and 700,000 at the time of Julius Caesar's visit (47 B.C.). If Cleopatra did receive Marc Antony's promised gift of the collection at Pergamum, then the highest figure reported for Alexandria, 900,000, may have been attained. Statistics, especially of books in libraries, often are suspect; and in any discussion of the size of Greek and Roman libraries, it should be explained that the typical ancient papyrus roll contained about one-seventh of the text of our ordinary book. In other words, the Alexandrian Library contained at its peak the equivalent of between 100,000 and 125,000 of today's volumes.

This, for the ancient world, was an enormous accumulation of books, and the amassing thereof required large expenditures of money and effort. Manuscripts were purchased in the book markets of Athens and Rhodes, and the books which came on ships to the harbor of Alexandria were confiscated. According to a famous story, Ptolemy III borrowed the best versions of the tragedies of Aeschylus, Sophocles, and Euripides from the Athenian state archives and left fifteen talents (about $45,000) as a pledge for their restitution. The originals were to be copied for the Alexandrian Library and then returned to Athens. "The king, however, sent back the copy instead of the original, and forfeited his pledge (not to mention his honour)."

Although the Hellenistic World embraced Greece and Macedonia in Europe, Egypt in Africa, and Asia Minor, its largest library contained few books in languages other than Greek. Copies of various editions of the major and minor works from Homer to Callimachus were in the Alexandrian Library, and here were the treatises of Archimedes, Euclid, and other Greek scientists. Books about other civilizations, such as Manetho's history of Egypt and Berossos' history of Babylon, were studied in the Museum, but their authors wrote in Greek. Numerous tongues were spoken on the streets and in the harbor of the capital of Ptolemaic Egypt, yet the Greek intellectuals who resided there appear not to have read them. The evidence is inconclusive, but the books written at Alexandria during the Hellenistic Age show no familiarity with foreign literatures and we know that much of the *Old Testament* was translated before 130 B.C. because the Hebraic characters could not be read by later learned Greeks.

Probably the best indication of the high place held by the Alexandrian Library in the Hellenistic World is the calibre of the men who directed its affairs. No other library, and few institutions of any kind, can match the distinction of the men connected with the largest library of the ancient world during its first one hundred and fifty years. Although the role of the founder, Demetrius of Phaleron, is hard to document, the names of the first six head librarians and of several assistants are known from a contemporary papyrus found in 1903–04 at Oxyrhynchus on the edge of the Libyan Desert. According to some accounts, Callimachus was head of the Library from 260 to 240 B.C., but others question whether he held any office in the institution. At least two of his students, including Eratosthenes who discovered a remarkably accurate means of measuring the circumference of the earth, held the post of librarian, and the teacher listed the manuscripts in his *Pinakes* (Tables) which filled 120 rolls. Callimachus is credited with having cataloged about a fifth of the

contents of the Alexandrian Library, but no part of his compilation survives. Despite this loss, Callimachus' fame is secure: he
deserves to be remembered both as the Father of Bibliography
and as the leading poet of ancient Alexandria. Callimachus'
erudition might occasionally chill a line ("I sing nothing that
is not attested"), yet he could and did write hauntingly beautiful verse:

"They told me, Heraclitus, they told me you were dead."

In addition to listing the collections, the scholars associated with
the Alexandrian Library undertook to edit the manuscripts in
their custody. This was an essential labor because of the nature
of the books published in the ancient world. If the author's auto-
graph of a book could be consulted, the proper text could be
established without difficulty; but most ancient books were
copied from the original or from other copies. Each time a book
was reproduced new errors were made, and, if numerous copies
were made from dictation by scribes, the errors multiplied. Accordingly, when several versions of a text were brought together
in an ancient library, the need for a reconciliation of the dis-
crepancies was obvious. Consequently, the librarians of the
Alexandrian Library addressed themselves to this arduous task,
and the editions they produced established the canons of the
major Greek writers.

The true Alexandrian period ended with the reign of the
fourth Ptolemy (205 B.C.), and after Ptolemy VI (145) Egypt
rapidly decayed. The charms of Cleopatra, the last of the Ptolemies, could not melt Octavian, and Egypt became in 30 B.C. a
province of Rome. Alexandria became the second city of the
Empire, and its Museum and Library probably survived the first
political shocks and disturbances. Julius Caesar is said to have
destroyed much of the Library through firing the docks at Alexandria in 47 B.C.; and Marc Antony is credited with having presented to Cleopatra the library of the kings of Pergamum which
contained 200,000 rolls. These may have been delivered, but, if
they were, it is not known where this collection was housed.
Uncertainties multiply because a second library was formed in

the temple of Serapis, and later chroniclers do not distinguish between the mother and the daughter libraries. The best educated guess is that the Museum Library did not survive Julius Caesar's conflagration and that the Serapeum Library did not survive the razing of the temple by Christians in A.D. 391. No document of the fifth, sixth, or early seventh centuries mentions a public library in Alexandria; consequently, it seems reasonable to conclude that none existed there after the fourth century.

When Alexandria fell to the Moslems on September 28, 642, 'Amr ibn al' Asi and his band of rude desert warriors were amazed at the size and splendor of their prize. The new conquerors were dazzled by the brightness of the sun on the white marble which abounded in pavements, buildings, and columns; so much so, wrote one imaginative Moslem, "it was painful to go out by night: for the moonlight reflected from the white marble made the city so bright that a tailor could see to thread his needle without a lamp." The number of baths and theaters which 'Amr captured in Alexandria was multiplied tenfold in later accounts, and five centuries after his conquest there appears for the first time the famous story of the burning of the Alexandrian Library which is too good to let die. It goes like this:

Shortly after the Muslims occupied Alexandria, a defrocked Coptic priest called John the Grammarian became acquainted with 'Amr, and each enjoyed the intellectual attainments and company of the other. After the two had become friendly, John broached a new subject: "You have examined the whole city, and have set your seal on every kind of valuable: I make no claim for aught that is useful to you, but things not useful to you may be of service to us."

"What are you thinking of?" asked 'Amr.

"The books of wisdom which are in the imperial treasuries," answered the Grammarian.

"That," responded 'Amr, "is a matter on which I can give no order without the authority of the Caliph."

'Amr sent an appropriate letter to the Caliph, and in due time Omar made this answer, "Touching the books you mention, if what is written in them agrees with the Book of God (the

Koran), they are not required: if it disagrees, they are not desired. Destroy them therefore."

Thereupon 'Amr ordered the books to be used for fuel for heating the baths of Alexandria, and the quantity of books was so great that six months were required to consume them.

In conclusion, the thirteenth-century Arab storyteller admonishes, "Listen and wonder."

The Abu 'l Faraj' tale has traveled far and wide although it is patently false; for example, John the Grammarian had died long before the Muslims invaded Egypt. Moreover, a careful sifting of the evidence indicates that although private libraries existed in Alexandria immediately before and after the Arab conquest in 642, the great public libraries had disappeared two centuries earlier. If any large Alexandrian libraries had flourished in the early seventh century, the books would have been removed during the armistice of eleven months which immediately preceded the entrance of 'Amr and his band into the city. Books were relatively higher priced then than now, and if any had remained during the year 641 in public libraries in Alexandria the volumes would have been shipped by sea for sale in other great cities of the Christian world. Indeed, there are reports—also unsubstantiated—that vast quantities of books were transported in the fourth century from Alexandria to Rome and Constantinople.

The uncertainty and confusion which surround the great library or libraries at Alexandria have a simple explanation: the necessary archaeological excavations have been few in number and limited in scope. The ruins of the old city lie below sea level directly beneath modern Alexandria, and drainage problems and high property values have deterred archaeologists from digging intensively in the locality. Ancient Alexandria, with its half million Macedonians, Greeks, Jews, Egyptians, Persians, Syrians, Arabs, and Negroes was truly "the city of the world," but nothing of it is to be seen today except a few catacombs, pillars, and minor relics. Traces of the imposing lighthouse on the island of Pharos which welcomed sea-weary travelers to Alexandria can still be found, but even the site of "the vast buttressed walls of the Library" remains uncertain.

Recovery of volumes from the Alexandrian Library is further complicated by the fact that most were papyrus rolls. Other writing materials used in the Greek and Roman worlds include small pieces of baked clay, prepared skins, and the waxed surfaces of wooden tablets, but papyrus was supreme until the end of the third century A.D. This writing material was made by pressing together two layers of strips of the papyrus plant which had been laid at right angles to each other. The material is durable under certain favorable conditions found in parts of Egypt, and numerous papyrus rolls have survived. But papyrus is soon destroyed by dampness, and this circumstance has caused scholars to conclude that it would be futile to make an attempt to recover papyrus rolls from the ruins of the library in Alexandria. Papyri written in Alexandria have been found in places where they had been taken in antiquity, but no fragment of papyrus has been recovered from the soil at the Delta of the Nile.

I cannot refute the opinions of experts in papyrology and Greco–Roman archaeology, but in this instance zeal and enthusiasm are preferable to professional expertise. The point at which the two broad and colonnaded thoroughfares crossed in ancient Alexandria has been identified in the modern city, and nearby under the Mosque of the Prophet Daniel reputedly are the tombs of Alexander and of some of the Ptolemies. Carefully made maps locate the Museum and its Library close by the tomb of Alexander, and opposite the Mosque stands a row of antique columns which may have formed part of the Museum's facade. This surely is the spot where new digging should begin.

The sandy soil of Alexandria has yielded coins with portraits of the Ptolemies, busts of Alexander in marble and in granite, statues of bulls, scarabs, and serpents, and marble sarcophagi. Should we not therefore continue to hope that an excavation at the site of Alexander's tomb might unearth the carved marble sarcophagus which contained the hero's body tightly bound in strips of hammered gold and at least one manuscript from the Museum Library which reposes unharmed in a sealed container?

Figure 1 Storage Bucket with Papyrus Rolls

Figure 2 Double Ink Stand and Reed Pen

Figure 3 Papyrus Roll Showing Title Label

Figure 4 Papyrus Roll Partially Unrolled

Plate II Roman Writing Equipment and Manuscript Books

ROMAN LIBRARIES

Under the Caesars books became inexpensive and were shipped from Rome to all parts of the Empire, or were published simultaneously in Rome, Lyons, Athens, or Alexandria. Private and public libraries were formed and maintained for display and for use, and at least two of the emperors, Domitian in the first century and Diocletian in the third, sent scribes to the Alexandrian Museum to copy books for the shelves at Rome. Literary culture flourished throughout the Empire in the second century after Christ. According to Chester G. Starr in Civilization and the Caesars (Ithaca: Cornell University Press, 1954), p. 238:

> The spread of the Greek and Latin languages in the East and West, the wide circulation of literary works and the foundation of libraries, the truly remarkable extent of literacy in the cities of the Empire—all these are marks of the attention which men paid to their intellectual heritage. The thinkers may not have thought as well, but more persons made the pretense of thinking—and their reflections were transmitted more widely and more speedily than ever before in human history.

In the essay which follows, I have attempted to show the vigor of classical civilization as it manifested itself in Roman libraries.

UNDER THE EMPERORS

The imagined charms of Helen of ancient Troy, her "hyacinth hair, classic face, and Naiad airs," transported the habitually morbid Edgar Allan Poe

> To the glory that was Greece,
> And the grandeur that was Rome.

Poe's uncharacteristic and oft-repeated lines suggest that Greece's glory and Rome's grandeur were constants, like Helen's beauty, but the suggestion is false. Greek civilization flamed for a few centuries in Athens and in distant Alexandria and Syracuse, yet by the time of Christ the hot fire had cooled to a warm glow and Greece's glory was overlain by Rome's grandeur. The two civilizations joined to form the pagan world, yet each kept its identity. Greece's literary and artistic creations were never equalled by Rome, but the latter surpassed the former in engineering, in law, and in administration. The Roman genius stands today among the ruins of the city of Timgad in North Africa, where the imperial legions built homes, streets, drains, temples, baths, and a forum, and inscribed on the forum's pavement, "To hunt, bathe, play, and laugh, this is to live." True, Timgad had a library, but this outpost of the Empire was not founded until the second century after Christ. During the five centuries in which Rome was built and Italy conquered, the Romans lived without libraries.

After Hannibal, the scourge of Italy, had been defeated at Zama in North Africa (202 B.C.), the Romans overwhelmed one of the Carthaginian's former allies, Philip V of Macedon, but, as Horace observed, "Conquered Greece took captive her barbarous conqueror." T. Quinctius Flaminius, the victorious Roman general, was a lover of Hellenism, and instead of destruction he offered freedom to the vanquished. The peace was broken by Philip's son Perseus, who was defeated in 168 B.C. at Pydna by another admirer of Greek culture, Lucius Aemilius Paullus. Perseus was taken to Rome as a captive, and with him as hostages went a thousand Greek leaders, including the historian Polybius. Thus began an invasion of scholars, tutors, philosophers, and artists who converted stoic Rome to Grecian ideals and Eastern luxury. Greece soon disappeared as a political power, but her culture came to dominate Western civilization through the might of her conqueror, Rome.

Among the plunder brought from the East by the Roman conquerors were great quantities of books, which gave rise to libraries at home. The library of the captive king of Macedon was kept by Aemilius Paullus as a heritage for his children, and almost a century later (86 B.C.), Sulla, another lover of Greece, conquered Athens and sent home the remnants of Aristotle's famous library. These and other books which Sulla had seized in the East were used after his death by Cicero, who also was enamored of both books and Greece. Lucius Licinius Lucullus, whose name is identified today with luxurious living, first won fame through an arduous eight-year campaign in Asia Minor, and, after his return to Rome, he understandably turned to pleasures provided by his patrimony and the spoils of war. Plutarch, who immortalized Lucullus's table, makes the point, "His furnishing a library, however, deserves praise and record, for he collected very many and choice manuscripts." Lucullus's library was open at all times, and the reading rooms and nearby walks were frequented by Greeks "whose delight it was to leave their other occupations and hasten thither as to the habitation of the Muses." The Roman generals who were Hellenists treasured books in Greek, but their interest in literature did not embrace the records of less congenial civilizations. The manners and customs of the Punic-speaking peoples meant little or nothing to the Romans, for they gave to their African allies the libraries of the doomed city of Carthage.

The examples of Aemilius Paullus, Sulla, and Lucullus in bringing to Rome books which would be used by others were improved on by Gaius Asinius Pollio, who created a library out of the spoils of the Dalmatian campaign fought in 39 B.C. When Caesar died, Pollio, who had crossed the Rubicon with him, was left stranded in Farther Spain, at the head of an army. After more than a year of watchful waiting, Pollio joined Antony against the Republicans, and his military fortunes reached their zenith when he conquered Dalmatia and returned to Rome in triumph. Pollio's triumph gave him the means to become a patron of poets, Horace and Vergil included, a writer of plays and histories, and the founder of a library. In 37 B.C., Pollio rebuilt and equipped the old Atrium Libertatis and placed therein collections of Greek and Latin books and busts of famous writers. The arrangements in the Atrium Libertatis were followed in the public libraries established under Augustus, but this does not justify identifying Pollio as the founder of the first public library in ancient Rome. This false attribution persists because of uncritical readings of the elder Pliny's eloquent statement that Asinius Pollio was "the first to make men's talents public property by dedicating a library."

Before the end of the Republic (30 B.C.), literature was fully domiciled in Rome. Cicero had a library in each of his villas, and he often wrote about books to his Athenian friend and publisher, Titus Pomponius Atticus. Two of Atticus's slaves were borrowed by Cicero to assist his slave in the arrangement of his books at his villa at Antium, and their work delighted him: "Since Tyrranio has arranged my books for me, my house seems to have a soul added to it." Cicero's enjoyment of books was not exceptional, and before long a library was essential in the home of every distinguished Roman. Banished Ovid was wretched without his books, and Horace would not go to the country he celebrated without his favorite volumes. In writing his Natural History, the elder Pliny consulted 2,000 volumes, most of which were in his own collection, and he employed every free moment, even at the baths, in reading.

In the reign of Augustus, Rome had its own book market, the Argiletum. Books were exported to all parts of the Empire, and Rome rivaled Alexandria as the literary capital of the Western world. Small books were advertised for sale for as little as fifty cents, and sumptuous copies were made to order. The fashion of collecting books for decorative purposes grew among the wealthy, until Seneca, the dramatist and tutor of Nero, was moved to satirize those who acquired books for display rather than for study. Seneca's barbs must have missed the Roman bibliophiles, for they were the subject of Lucian's ridicule in the second century and of Ausonius's in the fourth. John Evelyn's translation of Ausonius's epigram on the folly of book collecting should be better known:

> That thou with Books thy Library hast fill'd,
> Think'st thou thy self learn'd, and in Grammar skill'd?
> Then stor'd with Strings, Lutes, Fiddle-sticks now bought;
> Tomorrow thou Musitian may'st be thought.[4]

Although Julius Caesar is said to have planned to open to the public the greatest possible libraries of Greek and Latin books, the fulfillment thereof was realized first by his adopted son and heir, Octavian, who, in 27 B.C., became Augustus, the first of the Roman emperors. With his reign began the Pax Romana, a long period of unparalleled peace and prosperity, during which men of wealth and position generously supported games and public works, including libraries. The future first emperor founded the Octavian Library in 33 B.C. and the Palatine in 28 B.C., and this lead was followed by his successors, Tiberius, Vespasian, and Trajan. Trajan founded the Ulpian Library, the fame of which in antiquity was exceeded only by that of the libraries

---

[4] As quoted in Raymond Irwin, *The Origins of the English Library* (London: George Allen and Unwin, 1958), p. 133.

at Alexandria and Pergamum. Domitian, emperor from A.D. 81–96, rebuilt the libraries destroyed by fire in A.D. 80, and renewed their contents by sending scribes to Alexandria to copy manuscripts. The Palatine Library, which had burned in A.D. 192, was restocked in the third century A.D. by Gordian II from the 62,000 volumes amassed by his former tutor. Despite fires and time's vicissitudes, twenty-eight public libraries were counted in a fourth-century survey of notable buildings in Rome.

It is clear from inscriptions that the public libraries in Rome were linked together and administered by officials responsible to the emperor. The number of persons who worked in the Roman libraries cannot be ascertained, but in Tiberius's reign there were enough library employees for the emperor to appoint a physician to look after their health. The director of all the libraries was a "procurator," whose salary was less than that of other officers of his rank, for then, as now, distinguished librarians enjoyed considerable prestige but modest pay. Under the procurator, each institution was headed by a librarian who had charge of a corps of assistants and copyists. We know the identity of a few of the Roman librarians, and their careers suggest that learning and expertness were not uncommon in the public libraries of the Empire. Two of the librarians under Augustus, C. Julius Hyginus and Caius Melissus, won esteem as scholars before they were placed in charge of libraries, and the epigrammatist Martial, with a poet's flair for exaggeration, credited Sextus, then librarian at the Palatine, with "intelligence approaching that of a god."

The collections in the libraries in the Roman Empire seldom contained volumes in languages other than Latin and Greek, but the range of subjects covered was extremely wide. Ovid, the great Latin poet, wrote of the Palatine Library, "Whatsoever men, both formerly and now, have learnedly conceived lies open to the perusal of readers." Here, according to Suetonius, were the famous Sibylline Books in two gilded receptacles below the statue of Apollo. Other writers refer to volumes of poetry, law, history, biography, and oratory, and to files of public documents in the Roman libraries. Most of the volumes were papyrus rolls, but by the third century the codex had become common. The codex was superior to the roll for legal and other works which had to be consulted repeatedly, and the obvious advantages of

the new form—comprehensiveness, ease of reference, and durability—
led to its rapid adoption by the early Christians for religious works. In
the fourth century, vellum—finely prepared skins of animals—replaced
papyrus as the principal material for book production, hence, the form
of the typical medieval book, the vellum codex, was a bequest from
Rome.

The books in the Roman libraries could be read and consulted in
reading rooms or borrowed for use elsewhere, and the institutions
served as places for meetings of literary, social, and political groups.
The everyday use of the collections can be glimpsed in revealing anecdotes. In one of these, the author, Aulus Gellius, was with friends in
the little village of Tibur, and their conversation turned to whether
water condensed from snow, which they were then drinking, was
harmful. A member of the group recalled that Aristotle had condemned the drinking of this kind of water, and the speaker supported
his contention with the pertinent passage in a copy of the philoso-
pher's works which he fetched from the Tibur Library. Other Latin
writers made frequent use of books and documents in the public
libraries, and for his histories Vopiscus regularly drew on three of the
collections. His familiarity with their contents is revealed in his reference to a document signed by Emperor Tacitus in a book of ivory in
"the sixth armarium" (bookcase) at the Ulpian Library.

Although not one Roman library escaped destruction, a picture of
the physical arrangements can be formed from contemporary accounts
and from extant ruins. The typical structure included a portico for
reading, an entrance hall decorated with busts of famous writers, and
rooms for book storage. Separate apartments were provided for books
in Latin and for those in Greek, and the rolls were stored in cylinder-
shaped boxes or in cupboard-like bookcases. The book rooms faced the
east so that dampness, which was ruinous to papyrus and parchment,
could be kept to a minimum. Rome's public libraries were located
near temples or palaces and were joined to them by rows of columns;
because of this they were made of fine materials and must have presented a handsome appearance.

Older libraries in Greece and in Alexandria probably influenced the
physical arrangements of the public libraries in Rome, for similarities
between the ruins of the library excavated at Pergamum and those

unearthed at Rome indicate that the latter may have been formed along Greek lines. Indeed, Pergamum may have become the model for Roman libraries as early as 159 B.C., when Eumenes II, King of Pergamum, sent his librarian, Crates of Mallus, as envoy to Rome. Almost three centuries later, when the Emperor Hadrian, a brilliant Hellenist, set about to restore Athens, he constructed a library "with marble walls, 120 columns, a gilded roof, and spacious rooms sparkling with alabaster, paintings, and statuary."[5] If such a structure had been inappropriate, it probably would not have been built in Athens by the Emperor who was to reconstruct the Pantheon and to rebuild Rome.

Rome fell to the barbarians in the fifth century, because the vigor of her civilization had expired in the fourth. Greek Epicurianism, which had replaced the stern ethics of the Roman farmer–soldier of the early Republic, could not withstand either the pagan or the Christian excesses of the late Empire. When the Emperor Constantine embraced the new faith and made Constantinople his capital (A.D. 330), the center of Western civilization departed from Rome. At the end of the fourth century, Ammianus Marcellinus, last of the great Latin historians, saw in Rome "nothing save dissensions, taverns, and other similar vulgarities." The temper which had won renown by fierce wars was gone, and the Romans in A.D. 378, were addicted to gluttonous banquets and sluggish indolence. Ammianus, in his History, vol. 1, trans. by John C. Rolfe (Cambridge: Harvard University Press, 1935), p. 47, continued:

> In short, in place of the philosopher the singer is called in, and in place of the orator the teacher of stagecraft, and while the libraries are shut up forever like tombs, water-organs are manufactured and lyres as large as carriages, and flutes and huge instruments for gesticulating actors.

Ammianus Marcellinus's valedictory to the Roman libraries was premature, for the Ulpian survived the Vandal sack in A.D. 455, but by the fifth century the Romans had little need for libraries. Whether the many fine collections then in existence were destroyed by invaders, carried away in the seventh century to Constantinople, or simply perished from neglect must be left to conjecture. By the sixth century,

5 Will Durant, Caesar and Christ: A History of Roman Civilization and of Christianity from Their Beginnings to A.D. 325 (New York: Simon and Schuster, 1944), p. 418.

the forces which had created Greco–Roman civilization had burned out; how the charred fragments reached the modern world is part of the story of libraries during the Middle Ages.

EARLY CHRISTIAN LIBRARIES

Although Christianity became the state religion of Rome, paganism held on among the senatorial class, who worked to preserve the old gods and to preserve the classical literary heritage. When Gratian, who had studied under St. Ambrose, became emperor in 375, he ordered the removal of the statue of Victory and its altar from the Roman Senate. Symmachus, prefect of Rome and a leader of the senatorial aristocracy who cherished pagan culture, made an eloquent plea for their return. His words are quoted in Edward K. Rand's Founders of the Middle Ages, 2nd ed. (Cambridge: Harvard University Press, 1941), pp. 15–16:

> Grant, I implore you, that we who are old men may leave to posterity that which we received as boys. . . . All things are full of God, and no place is safe for perjurers, but the fear of transgression is greatly spurred by the consciousness of the very presence of deity. . . .
> . . . I do but ask peace for the gods of our fathers, the native gods of Rome. It is right that what all adore should be deemed one. We all look up at the same stars. We have a common sky. A common firmament encompasses us. What matters it by what kind of learned theory each man looketh for the truth? There is no one way that will take us to so mighty a secret. All this is matter of discussion for men of leisure. We offer your majesties not a debate but a plea.

But Christianity is not a tolerant religion, and St. Ambrose, in his response, would not allow that statues of the gods of "the cult that drove Hannibal from the walls of Rome and the Gauls from the Capitolium" belonged in the senate of a government which had an emperor who professed Christianity. The senatorial aristocracy lost the contest but their devotion to classical culture made possible the transmission to modern times of most of the Latin literature which has survived.

Most of the early Christian authors had attended traditional schools which followed a pattern of rhetorical training, with emphasis on the form and brilliance of classical literature. This posed for the educated Christian in the late Roman Empire a thorny problem in books and reading—could he enjoy pagan literature or should his reading be confined to the Scriptures and other sacred works? Tertullian, a North African theologian of the early third century, would have nothing to do with "wretched Aristotle," and the towering Origen sold his secular books because they were no longer of use to him. The conflict reached its most dramatic form in St. Jerome, who, although brought up as a Christian, had received the standard classical education. From it, he developed a love of learning and a devotion to scholarship which caused him to visit the educational centers of Gaul, Greece, and Asia Minor. In Rome, he had formed a library which he took with him to Jerusalem, where he worked and read until he became seriously ill. During this illness Jerome dreamed the famous dream which he recounted years later in a letter to a feminine correspondent. This version appears in Select Letters of St. Jerome, trans. by F. A. Wright (London: Heinemann, 1933), pp. 125–129 (reprinted with permission of the Loeb Classical Library and Harvard University Press).

> Many years ago for the sake of the kingdom of heaven I cut myself off from home, parents, sister, relations, and, what was harder, from the dainty food to which I had been used. But even when I was on my way to Jerusalem to fight the good fight there, I could not bring myself to forgo the library which with great care and labour I had got together at Rome. And so, miserable man that I was, I would fast, only to read Cicero afterwards. I would spend long nights in vigil, I would shed bitter tears called from my inmost heart by the remembrance of my past sins; and then I would take up Plautus again. Whenever I returned to my right senses and began to read the prophets, their language seemed harsh and barbarous. With my blind eyes I could not see the light: but I attributed the fault not to my eyes but to the sun. While the old serpent was thus mocking me, about the middle of Lent a fever attacked my weakened body and spread through my inmost veins. It may sound incredible, but the ravages it wrought on my unhappy frame were so persistent that at last my bones scarcely held together.
>
> Meantime preparations were made for my funeral: my whole

Plate III St. Jerome in His Cell

body grew gradually cold, and life's vital warmth only lingered faintly in my poor throbbing breast. Suddenly I was caught up in the spirit and dragged before the Judge's judgment seat: and here the light was so dazzling, and the brightness shining from those who stood around so radiant, that I flung myself upon the ground and did not dare to look up. I was asked to state my condition and replied that I was a Christian. But He who presided said: "Thou liest; thou art a Ciceronian, not a Christian. 'For where thy treasure is there will thy heart be also' "* Straightway I became dumb, and amid the strokes of the whip—for He had ordered me to be scourged—I was even more bitterly tortured by the fire of conscience, considering with myself the verse: "In the grave who shall give thee thanks?"† Yet for all that I began to cry out and to bewail myself, saying: "Have mercy upon me, O Lord, have mercy upon me": and even amid the noise of the lash my voice made itself heard. At last the bystanders fell at the knees of Him who presided, and prayed Him to pardon my youth and give me opportunity to repent of my error, on the understanding that the extreme of torture should be inflicted on me if ever I read again the works of Gentile authors. In the stress of that dread hour I should have been willing to make even larger promises, and taking oath I called upon His name: "O Lord, if ever again I possess worldly books or read them, I have denied thee."

After swearing this oath I was dismissed, and returned to the upper world. There to the surprise of all I opened my eyes again, and they were so drenched with tears, that my distress convinced even the incredulous. That this experience was no sleep nor idle dream, such as often mocks us, I call to witness the judgment seat before which I fell and the terrible verdict which I feared. May it never be my lot again to come before such a court as that! I profess that my shoulders were black and blue, and that I felt the bruises long after I awoke from my sleep. And I acknowledge that henceforth I read the books of God with a greater zeal than I had ever given before to the books of men.

* St. Matthew, vi. 21.
† Psalm vi. 5.

The struggle which gripped St. Jerome was resolved neatly by an eastern contemporary, St. Basil, who also had enjoyed a sound classical education in Caesaria, in Palestine, in Alexandria, and in Athens. Although Basil later reflected sourly on the "idle rapture" of his years in Athens, he enjoyed his familiarity with Plato, Homer, and other notable Greek writers. Basil did not ignore the dangers to be encountered in classical literature, but, as he counseled in his "Address to Young Men on Reading Greek Literature," in The Letters of Saint Basil, vol. 4, trans. by R. J. Deferrari and Martin McGuire (Cambridge: Harvard University Press, 1934), pp. 391–393, discriminating readers should reject the evil in pagan writings and hold fast to the good. In an oft quoted passage, Basil explained how this should be done:

> It is, therefore, in accordance with the whole similitude of the bees, that we should participate in the pagan literature. For these neither approach all flowers equally, nor in truth do they attempt to carry off entire those upon which they alight, but taking only so much of them as is suitable for their work, they suffer the rest to go untouched. We ourselves too, if we are wise, having appropriated from this literature what is suitable to us and akin to the truth, will pass over the remainder. And just as in plucking the blooms from a rose-bed we avoid the thorns, so also in garnering from such writings whatever is useful, let us guard ourselves against what is harmful.

By the middle of the fifth century, a Roman aristocrat could enjoy both pagan and Christian writers at his country villa. Sidonius Apollinaris and the other aristocrats in South Gaul had time on their hands, and they found amusement in literature and in parties.[6] One villa where Sidonius enjoyed his stay possessed handsome buildings, including a chapel and baths, carefully tended vineyards and orchards, and a well-stocked library to divert the master "between pen and plough."[7] At another villa Sidonius found young men playing ball in

---

[6] C. E. Stevens, *Sidonius Apollinaris and His Age* (Oxford: Clarendon Press, 1933), p. 14.

[7] *The Letters of Sidonius,* vol. 2, trans. by O. M. Dalton (Oxford: Clarendon Press, 1915), pp. 142–143.

one room, others at dice tables in a second, and books in "towering presses" in a third.[8] Manuscripts of a devotional type were located near the seats for ladies, and those by authors distinguished by the grandeur of Latin eloquence were near the gentlemen's benches. Both pagan and Christian authors were represented, for Sidonius and his friends were as ready to read literature for its artistry as for its expressions of faith. Indeed, Sidonius evidenced more interest in the quality of a Latin translation of Origen than in the ideas of the great theologian.

Christianity was rooted in Scriptures which had to be read, and this led to the multiplication and preservation of copies. Close study of the Scriptures prompted the publication of explanatory sermons and essays, and these in turn evoked responses, pro and con. By the end of the second century, learned Christians corresponded frequently about matters of doctrine and church administration, and it is indeed remarkable that many of their letters were preserved for at least a century in the earliest Christian library, that at Aelia (Jerusalem), founded in 212 by Bishop Alexander of that city. Eusebius tells us in his Historia Ecclesiastica (326) that in the library at Aelia he had gathered material "for this very work at hand." Better known is the Christian library at Caesarea with which Eusebius was closely connected. It is described in William E. Scudamore's "Libraries," in A Dictionary of Christian Antiquities, vol. 1, ed. by William Smith and Samuel Cheetham (Hartford, Conn.: J. B. Burr, 1880), p. 985:

> The most ancient library of Christian books mentioned by any historian is that at Aelia (Jerusalem), collected by Alexander, the bishop of that city, A.D. 212. Eusebius of Caesarea, writing about 330, says that it contained the epistles, from one to another, of many learned ecclesiastics of the time of Origen (A.D. 230), and that he had himself made very great use of it in compiling his history (Hist. Eccl. vi. 20). There was a much larger and more famous library at Caesarea in Palestine, which appears to have been founded by Origen, with the munificent aid, we may suppose, of his friend Ambrosius, and to have been greatly

---

[8] Sidonius: Poems and Letters, vol. 1, trans. by W. B. Anderson (Cambridge: Harvard University Press, 1936), pp. 453–455.

enlarged by Pamphilus, the friend of Eusebius, A.D. 294. That it existed before the time of Pamphilus is clear from St. Jerome's account: "Having sought for them (books) over the world, but devoting himself especially to the books of Origen, he gave them to the library at Caesarea: (*Expos. in Ps.* 126, *Ep.* 34 *ad Marcellam* (1).

The same author calls it the library of Origen and Pamphilus (*De Vir. Illust.* c. 113). In this library there was, as he informs us, the supposed Hebrew original of St. Matthew's Gospel (*ibid.* c. 3), which is probably the book (in the same collection) which he elsewhere describes as a Gospel in Syro-Chaldaic, used by the Nazarenes (*Contra Pelag.* iii. 2). In another work he says, "I have been somewhat diligent in searching for copies, and in the library of Eusebius at Caesarea I found six volumes of the *Apology* for Origen" (by Pamphilus) (*C. Rufin.* ii. 12). It contained copies of the greater part of the works of Origen, made by Pamphilus himself (Hieron. *de Vir. Illust.* c. 75). The originals of the Hexapla were there, and Jerome corrected his copy from them (*Comment.* in Tit. iii. 9). Before the time of Jerome this library had fallen more or less into decay, but endeavours to restore it were made by two successors of Eusebius, viz. Acacius, 340, and Euzoius, 366 (Hieron. *ad Marcell.* u. s.). Of Euzoius, he says, on the authority of Thespesius Rhetor, that he "strove with great labour to refurnish with parchments the library of Origen and Pamphilus, which was already decayed" (*De Vir. Illust.* c. 113). Isidore of Seville, A.D. 636, asserts that the library of Pamphilus at Caesarea contained nearly 30,000 volumes (*Orig.* vi. 6).

The library at Caesarea probably survived until the Saracens took the city early in the seventh century (638), for in 616–617, a Syrian Bishop made a translation from Origen's Hexapla (an edition of the Old Testament in six languages), which St. Jerome had consulted before the end of the fourth century.[9]

---

[9] Edgar J. Goodspeed, *A History of Early Christian Literature* (Chicago: University of Chicago Press, 1942), p. 245.

The Middle Ages

In old-fashioned textbooks the Middle Ages span the thousand years between the Fall of Rome (476) and the Fall of Constantinople (1453), a period which appears at first glance to be a cultural void between the classical achievements of the ancient world and the bright and vigorous era we call the Renaissance. A better understanding of the millennium between the ancient and modern periods can be had through thinking of these years not as a separate period, but as aspects of the end of the ancient world and of the beginning of the modern. The dividing line between the two falls at about the tenth century; the centuries between the sixth and the tenth are referred to as the Early Middle Ages or the Dark Ages, and the three centuries in which medieval civilization produced its Gothic cathedrals and other monuments are termed the Later (or High) Middle Ages. In this light therefore, medieval civilization begins with the establishment of Christianity, which occurred at the height of the Roman Empire, and the Bible ranks as the earliest of the modern books.

Although certain themes, such as the persistence of paganism, the growth of the organized Church, and the transformation of barbarian tribes into nationalistic states, continue throughout the Early Middle Ages, these centuries tend to be confusing because of their discontinuous character. While the reader of ancient history perceives civilization as moving forward under a succession of peoples, the disparateness of the five centuries between the end of the Roman Empire and the beginning of the High Middle Ages bewilders and wearies the uninitiated. The Early Middle Ages often seem to consist of a series of false starts; here are the examples furnished by the historian Christopher Dawson, in his Medieval Essays (London: Sheed and Ward, 1953), p. 117.

> Thus in Italy the work of Theodoric was undone by Justinian, and the work of Justinian by the Lombards; in Ireland and Northumbria the achievements of the new Christian culture were ruined by the Viking raiders; while the Carolingian Empire itself, the most imposing political creation of the early Middle Ages, is hardly established before it begins to fall to pieces, leaving Western Christendom more derelict and more devoid of order than ever before.

Although the end of the Roman Empire brought ruin to the public libraries and to collections belonging to nobles in Rome, classical literature did not completely disappear. Fragments of pagan culture were nurtured during the Dark Ages in isolated monasteries, but the mainstream of Greek letters flowed on for a thousand years in Constantinople, the eastern capital of the Empire. Masterpieces of ancient Greek fertilized medieval civilization among the Byzantines, and survived to stimulate learning among the Muslims and, centuries later, to reinvigorate Western Europe.

BYZANTINE LIBRARIES

Christianity had become the state religion of the Roman Empire under Constantine the Great, who, in 313, decreed freedom of religion in the Empire, and convened the Council of Nicea (325) to formulate Christian doctrine. Constantine built the city of Constantinople on the Bosporus, and there, in 330, he established his capital. The idea of a single Roman Empire continued for centuries, but the presence of barbarians on the frontiers, a fact which led to the founding of Constantinople, caused the Empire to split in twain. Greek and Latin manuscripts had been collected in the libraries of the early Roman Empire, but the division of the Empire divorced the two cultures. Medieval civilization in the West was built on the remnants of Latin culture; the civilization of the Eastern Empire, which lasted for a thousand years, was medieval Greek.

Education and letters were valued highly under the Byzantines, and schools were established for the instruction of the young. The Eastern court needed men trained in the professions, and this led to the founding of a university at Constantinople in 425. The Eastern Empire became involved in theological controversies which ultimately led, in the eleventh century, to a division of the Christian Church into the Orthodox and the Roman Catholic. The Byzantines loved theological arguments and ecclesiastical ceremonies, and these were encouraged in monasteries and in missionary work among the Slavs.

Medieval Byzantine culture flowered in the ninth, tenth, and eleventh centuries. Education among the Byzantines was based on the old Greek literature, and this led to textual and philological studies. Dictionaries and anthologies were compiled and copied. Photius's Myriobiblon, one of the few books from this civilization that is known in the West, contains brief abstracts of 279 literary and theological works which the writer, who had been sent as ambassador to Bagdad, prepared for his brother Tarasius at home. According to Photius's introductory letter, Tarasius had requested "summaries of those works which had been read and discussed during your absence." If we can believe Photius, he thereupon dictated to a secretary summaries of the exactly 279 books he could recall. This extraordinary communication between the two brothers is prized today by students of Byzantine civilization, since some of the works summarized therein have disappeared and would be unknown except for Photius's descriptions.

The study of Greek writers, pagan and Christian, and the compilation of manuals on nearly every conceivable subject required extensive libraries, and as a consequence, the Macedonian period (867–1056) was distinguished by great collections. Passing references to these are scattered among writings on the Byzantines, but it is very difficult to form a satisfactory notion of how books were used in the Eastern Empire. The fullest treatment, Joan M. Hussey's Church and Learning in the Byzantine Empire, 867–1185 names Byzantine authors such as Arethas of Caesarea, who studied and transcribed Greek writings,[10] but does not bring the subject of libraries into clear focus. Excerpts

[10] Joan M. Hussey, Church and Learning in the Byzantine Empire, 867–1185 (London: Oxford University Press, 1937), p. 35.

from an older essay, Frederic Harrison's Byzantine History in the Early Middle Ages (London: Macmillan, 1900), pp. 13–37, passim, offer a look at and an evaluation of the medieval civilization which had Constantinople as its home.

From the seventh to the thirteenth century Constantinople was far the largest, wealthiest, most splendid city in Europe. It was in every sense a new Rome. And, if it were at all inferior as a whole to what its mother was in the palmy age of Trajan and Hadrian, it far surpassed the old Rome in its exquisite situation, in its mighty fortifications, and in the beauty of its central palace and church. A long succession of poets and topographers have re-counted the glories of the great city—its churches, palaces, baths, forum, hippodrome, columns, porticoes, statues, theatres, hos-pitals, reservoirs, aqueducts, monasteries, and cemeteries. All accounts of early travellers from the West relate with wonder the splendour and wealth of the imperial city. "These riches and buildings were equalled nowhere in the world," says the Jew Benjamin of Tudela in the twelfth century. "Over all the land there are burghs, castles, and country towns, the one upon the other without interval," says the Saga of King Sigurd, fifty years earlier. The Crusaders, who despised the Greeks of the now de-cayed empire, were awed at the sight of their city; and as the pirates of the Fifth Crusade sailed up the Propontis they began to wonder at their own temerity in attacking so vast a fortress.

The dominant note of all observers who reached Constanti-nople from the North or the West, at least down to the eleventh century, even when they most despised the effeminacy and ser-vility of its Greek inhabitants, was this: they felt themselves in presence of a civilisation more complex and organized than any extant. It was akin to the awe felt by Goths and Franks when they first fell under the spell of Rome. At the close of the sixth century, as Dr. Hodgkin notes of Childebert's fourth invasion of Italy, "mighty were a few courteous words from the great Roman Emperor to the barbarian king"—the king whom Maurice the "Imperator semper Augustus" condescends to address as "vir gloriosus." And this idea that New Rome was the centre of the civilised world, that Western sovereigns were not their equals, lasted down to the age of Charles. When the Caroline Empire was decaying and convulsed, the same idea took fresh force. And the sense that the Byzantine world had a fulness and a culture which they had not, persisted until the Crusades effectually broke the spell.

This sentiment was based on two very real facts. The first was that New Rome prolonged no little of the tradition, civil and military organisation, wealth, art, and literature of the older Rome, indeed far more than remained west of the Adriatic. The second, the more important, and the only one on which I now desire to enlarge, was that, in many essentials of civilisation, it was more modern than the nascent nations of the West. Throughout the early centuries of the Middle Ages—we may say from the age of Justinian to that of Hildebrand—the empire on the Bosphorus perfected an administrative service, a hierarchy of dignities and offices, a monetary and fiscal system, a code of diplomatic formulas, a scientific body of civil law, an imperial fleet, engines of war, fortifications, and resources of maritime mobilisation, such as were not to be seen in Western kingdoms till the close of the Middle Ages, and which were gradually adopted or imitated in the West. At a time when Charles, or Capet, or Otto were welding into order their rude peoples, the traveller who reached the Bosphorus found most of the institutions and habits of life such as we associate with the great cities of much later epochs. He would find a regular city police, organised bodies of municipal workmen, public parks, hospitals, orphanages, schools of law, science, and medicine, theatrical and spectacular amusements, immense factories, sumptuous palaces, and a life which recalls the Cinque Cento in Italy. . . .

For the historian, the point of interest in this Byzantine administration is that, with all its crimes and pomposities, it was systematic and continuous. It never suffered the administrative and financial chaos which afflicted the West in the fifth century, or in the ninth century after the decay of the Carlings, and so on down to the revival of the Holy Roman Empire by Otto the Great. It is difficult to overrate the ultimate importance of the acceptance by Charles of the title of Emperor, or of its revival by Otto; and history has taken a new life since the modern school has worked out all that these meant to the West. But we must be careful not to fall into the opposite pitfall, as if the Roman Empire had been *translated* back again to the West, as some clerical enthusiasts pretended, as if the Empire of Charles was a continuous and growing organism from the time of Charles down to Rudolph of Hapsburg, or as if the coronation of Charles or of Otto at Rome broke the continuity of Empire at the Bosphorus, or even greatly diminished its authority and prestige. On the contrary, these Western ceremonies affected it only for a season, and from time to time, and affected its temper more than its power.

The Western Empire, for all the strong men who at times wielded its sceptre, and for the fitful bursts of force it displayed, was long before it quite recognised its own dignity and might; it was very vaguely and variously understood at first by its composite parts; and for the earlier centuries was a loose, troubled, and migratory symbol of rank rather than a fixed and recognised system of government. All this time the Emperors in the vermilion buskins were regularly crowned in the Holy Wisdom; they all worshipped there, and all lived and ruled under its shadow. Their palaces by the Bosphorus maintained, under every dynasty and through every century, the same vast bureaucratic machine, and organised from the same centre the same armies and fleets; they supported the same churches, libraries, monasteries, schools, and spectacles, without the break of a day, however much Muslim invaders plundered or occupied their Asiatic provinces, and although the rulers of Franks or Saxons defied their authority or borrowed their titles. The Empire of Franks and Teutons was not a systematic government and had no local seat. That of the Greeks, as they were called, had all the characters of a fixed capital and of a continuous State system. . . .

Turn to the history of Art. Here, again, it must be said that from the fifth to the eleventh century the Byzantine and Eastern world preserved the traditions, and led the development of art in all its modes. We are now free of the ancient fallacy that Art was drowned beneath the waves of the Teutonic invaders, until many centuries later it slowly came to life in Italy and then north of the Alps. The truth is that the noblest and most essential of the arts—that of building—some of the minor arts of decoration and ornament, and the art of music, down to the invention of Guido of Arezzo in the eleventh century, lived on and made new departures, whilst most of the arts of form died down under the combined forces of barbarian convulsions and religious asceticism. And it was Byzantium which was the centre of the new architecture and the new decoration, whilst it kept alive such seeds of the arts of form as could be saved through the rudeness and the fanaticism of the early Middle Ages. To the age of Justinian we owe one of the greatest steps ever taken by man in the art of building. The great Church of the Holy Wisdom exerted over architecture a wider influence than can be positively claimed for any single edifice in the history of the arts. We trace enormous ramifications of its example in the whole East and the whole of the West, at Ravenna, Kief, Venice, Aachen, Palermo, Thessalonica, Cairo, Syria, Persia, and Delhi. And with all the enthusiasm we must feel for the Parthenon and the Pantheon, for Amiens and Chartres, I must profess my personal conviction that the interior of Agia Sophia is the grandest in the world, and certainly that one which offers the soundest basis for the architecture of the future. . . .

It is the same in the art of illuminating manuscripts. Painting, no doubt, declined more rapidly than any other art under the combined forces of barbarism and the gospel. But from the fifth to the eleventh century the paintings in Greek manuscripts are far superior to those of Western Europe. The Irish and Caroline schools developed a style of fine calligraphy and ingenious borders and initials. But their figures are curiously inferior to those of the Byzantine painters, who evidently kept their borderings subdued so as not to interfere with their figures. Conservatism and superstition smothered and eventually killed the art of painting, as it did the art of sculpture, in the East. But there are a few rare manuscripts in Venice, in the Vatican, the French Bibliothèque Nationale—all certainly executed for Basil I., Nicephorus,

and Basil II in the ninth and tenth centuries—which in drawing,
even of the nude, in composition, in expression, in grandeur of
colour and effect, are not equalled until we reach the fourteenth
century in Europe. The Vatican, the Venice, and the Paris examples, in my opinion, have never been surpassed. . . .

We err also if we have nothing but contempt for the Byzantine intellectual movement in the early Middle Ages. It is dis-
paraged for two reasons—first, that we do not take account of the
only period when it was invaluable, from the eighth to the
eleventh centuries; and, secondly, because the Greek in which it
was expressed falls off so cruelly from the classical tongue we
love. But review the priceless services of this semibarbarous literature when literature was dormant in the West. How much
poetry, philosophy, or science was there in Western Europe between Gregory the Great and Lanfranc? A few ballads, annals,
and homilies of merit, but quite limited to their narrow locali-
ties. For the preservation of the language, literature, philosophy,
and science of Greece mankind were dependent on the Roman
Empire in the East, until the Saracens and Persians received and
transmitted the inheritance.

From the time of Proclus in the fifth century, there had never
been wanting a succession of students of the philosophers of
Greece; and it is certain that for some centuries the books and
the tradition of Plato and Aristotle were preserved to the world
in the schools of Alexandria, Athens, and then of Byzantium. Of
the study and development of the civil law we have already
spoken. And the same succession was maintained in physical science. Both geometry and astronomy were kept alive, though not
advanced. The immortal architects of the *Holy Wisdom* were
scientific mathematicians, and wrote works on Mechanics. The
mathematician Leo, in the middle of the ninth century, lectured
on Geometry in the Church of the Forty Martyrs at Constantinople, and he wrote an essay on Euclid, when there was little
demand for science in the West, in the age of Lewis the Pious
and the descendants of Ecgbert. In the tenth century we have an
essay on a treatise of Hero on practical geometry. And Michael
Psellus in the eleventh century, the "Prince of Philosophers,"

wrote, amongst other things, on mathematics and astronomy. From the fourth to the eleventh century we have a regular series of writers on medicine, and systematic treatises on the healing art. . . .

The peculiar, indispensable service of Byzantine literature was the preservation of the language, philology, and archaeology of Greece. It is impossible to see how our knowledge of ancient literature or civilisation could have been recovered if Constantinople had not nursed through the early Middle Ages the vast accumulations of Greek learning in the schools of Alexandria, Athens, and Asia Minor; if Photius, Suidas, Eustathius, Tzetzes, and the Scholiasts had not poured out their lexicons, anecdotes, and commentaries; if the *Corpus Scriptorum historiae Byzantinae* had never been compiled; if indefatigable copyists had not toiled in multiplying the texts of ancient Greece. Pedantic, dull, blundering as they are too often, they are indispensable. We pick precious truths and knowledge out of their garrulities and stupidities, for they preserve what otherwise would have been lost for ever. It is no paradox that their very merit to us is that they were never either original or brilliant. Their genius, indeed, would have been our loss. Dunces and pedants as they were, they servilely repeated the words of the immortals. Had they not done so, the immortals would have died long ago.

MUSLIM LIBRARIES

After the death in 632 of Muhammad, his Arab followers began a series of remarkable conquests which, within a few decades, extended from the Arabian Sea in the east and the Caspian in the north to Tripoli on the southern shore of the Mediterranean. Early in the eighth century, less than a hundred years after the Prophet's death, the Arab–Muslim empire reached from Central Asia southward into India, westward across North Africa, and thence northward into Spain. The conquerors converted the conquered to Islam, and were quick to adopt and employ the scientific achievements of the Hellenistic world. In the eighth and ninth centuries the Islamic world embraced Greek science, and many of its landmarks, documented in Greek, were translated into Arabic. Through care and study the Muslims preserved and advanced Greek accomplishments in natural science and philosophy, but chose to follow Persian models in the writing of history and belles lettres.

There are numerous references to books and libraries among the Muslims in the eighth, ninth, and tenth centuries, many of which are brought together in S. K. Padover's chapter on "Muslim Libraries" in James Westfall Thompson's The Medieval Library (Chicago: University of Chicago Press, 1939), pp. 347–368 (reprinted with permission of the present holder of the copyright)*:

> The Arabian domination over the last Persian Empire, which was completed in A.D. 641, brought Arabian culture directly into contact with the last Persian culture and soon conquered the conquerors. But Persian culture in the fifth and sixth centuries had already been deeply penetrated by Greek influences, so that it was actually a Graeco–Persian culture which finally prevailed over the Arabs. The intermediates in this transmission of Greek thought to the East were the Syrians. In the schools of Antioch, Berytus, and especially Edessa the chief works of Greek philosophy and science were translated into Syriac; but the Syrians were indifferent to Greek literature, grammar, and rhetoric. The Syrians were Nestorian Christians and, accordingly, were persecuted as schismatics, if not heretics, by the orthodox government of the Eastern Roman or Byzantine Empire, the policy of which was to impose rigid religious uniformity within the empire. In 487 the school at Edessa was closed by the emperor Zeno, and the exiled teachers were given asylum at Nisíbis, in the heart of the medieval Persian Empire.
>
> In the Byzantine Empire the orthdox government continued to tighten its grip upon the schools until the school at Athens remained the only place where unfettered pursuit of learning survived. The extinction of the Greek spirit and of Greek learning befell in 529, when the emperor Justinian closed the school at Athens. Then seven of the teachers there were exiled, and found refuge at the court of Noshirvan, the greatest ruler of the last

---

* The footnotes in this section are not sequential because the essay is not reprinted in its entirety. See The Medieval Library for complete documentation.

native dynasty of Persia, the Sassanid.[2] In the middle of the sixth century, Persia therefore became the repository of Greek philosophy and science, the cultivation of which all but perished in Europe.[3] Hundreds of translators, most of them Hellenized Syrians, were employed in translating the masterpieces of Greek thought into the Persian language. Thus it came about that, when the Arabs conquered Persia, they fell heir to the native Persian literature and science, on the one hand, and Persian–Greek philosophy and science on the other, all of which body of thought was speedily assimilated by them through translation into the Arabic language.[4] Hence, it followed that, when the Arabs became safely settled within the conquered territories and gradually imbibed the amenities of civilization, their libraries were filled with books of Persian literature and Greek philosophic and scientific thought, the only Arabic evidence in them being the language and script in which they were written.

It required nearly two hundred years of slow education, however, before the conquerors reached this state of mind. The Arabs had lived for centuries—perhaps even some thousands of years—in Arabia, isolated, except along the edges of their land, from contact with the outside world, without knowledge of writing and reading, and therefore ignorant of books and the lore of learning. Writing to the majority was a species of magical signs and reading the mummery of necromancy. Such inborn prejudices could not be exterminated in a day.[5] But gradually the pernicious tradition of exclusion and ignorance was broken down under the impact of Persian and Syro–Greek culture disseminated from Ctesiphon and Nisíbis.

The first Muslim ruler who evinced an eager interest in non-

---

[2] These seven were named Damascius, Simplicius, Eudalius, Periscianus, Hermias, Diogenes, and Isidorus.

[3] But Greek medicine may be said to have survived in science.

[4] On this process see W. Kusch, "Zur Geschichte der Syrier-Arabischen Uebersetzungsliteratur," Orientalia, VI (1937), 68–82. The great French scholar Ernest Renan was the first to perceive the importance of this Arabic literature.

[5] For this early Arabian distrust of writing and reading see S. Margoliouth, Lectures on Arabic Historians (Calcutta, 1930), pp. 42–47. But see F. Krenkow, "The Use of Writing for the Preservation of Ancient Arabic Poetry," A Volume of Oriental Studies Presented to E. G. Browne (Cambridge, 1922), pp. 261 ff.

Arabian culture was the caliph Al-Mamum (813–33), of Bagdad, who gathered around him a great number of Syrian translators and scribes, who converted into Arabic the Greek–Syriac–Persian works which the Arabs had found in fallen Persia. One of the greatest of these translators was Ayyub al-Ruhawi, or Job of Edessa (ca. 760–835), a Nestorian Syrian. He was a prolific writer, but only two of his works have come down—a treatise on canine hydrophobia and an encyclopedia of philosophical and natural science entitled *The Book of Treasures.*[6] Another famous Syrian adapter or translator of works of Greek science was Hunayn ibn Ishaq (809–77), whose son and nephew followed in his steps. He translated the works of Hippocrates and Galen, and with him the history of Arabian medicine may be said to begin. Following him came al-Razi, known to western Europe later as "Rhazes." He was an Arabized Persian and the greatest physician of the Muslim world, the author of over two hundred works in medicine. Unfortunately, the original Greek texts from which these translations were made, were destroyed, so that the Greek texts themselves were not recovered in many instances until after 1204, when Constantinople fell into the hands of the crusaders.[7] The sack of the greatest capital of Christendom resulted in a prodigious number of manuscripts of all sorts being dispersed, many of which slowly found their way west for years afterward.

For four hundred years Arabian science, of mingled Greek, Persian, and Hindu elements, continued to flourish and expand over the Muslim world, and private and school libraries in Islam were crowded with these works. Of hardly less radius was the spread of Old Persian literature in the new guise of the Arabic language. As the chief names in the history of Muslim science are those of Arabized Syrians and Jews, so the chief names in the history of Arabic literature are those of Arabized Persians. Just as Latin literature drew so heavily upon Greek literature, both for themes and forms, so Arabic literature imitated Old Persian literature.

[6] The Arabic text is lost, but the Syriac version was edited and translated by A. Mingana ("Woodbrooke Scientific Publications," I [Cambridge, 1935]). For a review see *Isis,* XXV (1936), 141–44.

[7] A. H. L. Heeren, *Geschichte der classischen Literatur im Mittelalter,* I, 152–56.

Creative authorship and erudite scholarship were treated with admiration and reverence in the Muslim world when culture was at its height in the eleventh and twelfth centuries, libraries were numerous, and there was a flourishing book trade. When, in the former century, a distinguished theologian traveled through Persia, all the people in every village thronged to see him. Merchants and artisans threw their wares in his path; sweets and fine cloths were given him; flowers were showered upon him.[8]

Bagdad in its glory abounded with libraries. Even before the caliph al-Mamun, in the time of his father, Harun al-Rashid, the Arabian historian Omar al-Waqidi (736–811) possessed one hundred and twenty camel loads of books.[9] Al-Mamun's "house of wisdom" was founded shortly after A.D. 813; the vizier Ardashir (1024) established the "house of learning" about 991; the Nizamiyah madrasah, or college, was founded in 1064; the Mustansiriyah madrasah in 1233, just twenty-five years before the destruction of Bagdad by the Mongols.[10] These were great collections and of a semipublic nature. But there were many private libraries, as we know from the list, or *Fihrist*,[11] compiled about A.D. 987 by al-Nadim, the son of a bookseller. He was himself probably a bookseller, judging from the nature and extent of his references to books, authors, and the book trade. The scholar al-Baiquani (1033) had so many books that it required sixty-three hampers and two trunks to transport them. Another famous bibliophile was Mohammed ben al-Husain of Haditha, who was a friend of the author of the *Fihrist*. His collection of rare manuscripts was so precious that it was kept under lock and key. . . .

Every important city in Persia had its library.[21] . . . Book col-

---

[8] A. Mez, *Die Renaissance des Islams* (Heidelberg, 1922), pp. 163–164.

[9] Margoliouth, *op. cit.*, 192; A. Grohmann, "Bibliotheken und Bibliophilen im islamischen Orient," *Festschrift der Nationalbibliothek in Wien* (Vienna, 1926), p. 439.

[10] O. Pinto, "The Libraries of the Arabs during the Time of the Abassids," *Islamic Culture*, III (1929), 223–24.

[11] Ed. G. Flügel (Leipzig, 1871–72); R. A. Nicholson, *A Literary History of the Arabs* (Cambridge, 1930), pp. 361–64.

[21] See E. Herzfeld, "Einige Bücherschätze in Persien," *Ephemerides orientales* (Leipzig, 1926), No. 28, pp. 1–8.

lections were to be found in Nishapur, Ispahan, Ghaznah, Basrah, Shiraz, Merv, and Mosul. In Mosul the poet Ibn Hamdan (d. 935) founded a house of learning and stocked it with books on all branches of knowledge. It was open to all scholars, and those who were poor were given paper free. Basrah, famous for its grammarians, [22] had a library built by the courtier Adud el-Daulah (d. 982), where those who read or copied received a stipend.[23] In Ispahan a rich landowner established a library in 885 and is said to have spent 300,000 dirhems on books.[24] Ibn Hibban (d. 965), the qadi of Nishapur, bequeathed to his city a house with a "library and quarters for foreign students and provided stipends for their maintenance." Books were not to be loaned out.[25]

Of the Persian libraries, perhaps the best were those of Shiraz and Merv. The Shiraz foundation was built by the Buyyid prince Adud ad-Daula (d. 982) on his palace grounds. The library, which contained much scientific literature, was in charge of a director (wakil), a librarian (hazin), and a superintendent (muskrif). The books were stored in a long, arched hall, with stack rooms on all sides. Against the walls stood bookpresses, six feet high and three yards wide, made of carved wood, with doors which closed from the top down, each branch of knowledge having separate bookcases and catalogues.[26] . . .

The great Moslem civilization in the East was finally crushed by the invading hordes of Mongols and Tatars, culminating, in 1258, when Hulagu Khan sacked Bagdad. "They came," a contemporary says of the Mongols, "they uprooted, they burned, they slew, they carried off, they departed." Neither Genghiz Khan nor Hulagu Khan had any regard for human life or institutions of culture. They stabled their horses in mosques; burned libraries; used precious manuscripts for fuel; and razed con-

[22] Cambridge Medieval History (New York, 1923), IV, 291.
[23] Pinto, op. cit., pp. 224–25.
[24] S. Khuda Bukhsh, "The Renaissance of Islam," Islamic Culture, IV (1930), 295.
[25] Ibid., p. 297; Grohmann, op. cit., p. 441.
[26] Von Kremer, op. cit., II, 483–84; Grohmann, op. cit., pp. 436–37; Pinto, op. cit., p. 228.

quered cities, with their populations, to the ground. In the sack of Bukhara 30,000 people were slain. Of all the Mongols, only Timur (or Timurlane) had some respect for the literature of the conquered people. He collected many books and built a large library in his capital at Samarkand.[30] . . .

The first library in Cairo was established by the Fatimid caliph Al-Aziz (975–96) in 988, in connection with his house of learning, where thirty-five students were supported from endowments.[34] This school library had perhaps 100,000 volumes (some say 600,000) of bound books, among which were 2,400 Korans beautifully illuminated in gold and silver and stored in a separate room above the library proper. The rest of the books—on jurisprudence, grammar, rhetoric, history, biography, astronomy, and chemistry—were kept in large presses around the walls, which were divided into shelves, each of which had a door with a lock. Over the door of each section was nailed a list of all the books contained therein, as well as a notice of the lacunae in each branch of knowledge.[35]

A large part of this collection went into the "house of science," or "house of wisdom," founded by Caliph Al-Hakim in 1004, which acquired so vast a collection of rare books that legend exaggerated its number to 1,600,000 books.

> On the 8th day of Jumada II, 395 A.H. (1004 A.D.), was opened the building called the House of Wisdom. The students took up their residence. The books were brought from the libraries of the garrisoned Castles (the residences of the Fatimid Caliphs) and the public was admitted. Whoever wanted was at liberty to copy any book he wished to copy, or whoever required to read a certain book found in the library could do so. Scholars studied the Koran, astronomy, grammar, lexicography and medicine. The building was, moreover, adorned by carpets, all doors and corridors had curtains, and managers, servants, porters and other menials were appointed to maintain the establishment. Out of the

[30] Browne, op. cit., II, 12.
[34] Pinto, op. cit., p. 225.
[35] Grohmann, op. cit., p. 432.

library of the Caliph al-Hakim those books were brought
. . . , books in all sciences and literatures and of exquisite
calligraphy such as no other king had ever been able to
bring together. Al-Hakim permitted admittance to everyone, without distinction of rank, who wished to read or
consult any of the books.[36] . . .

In 1068, some sixty years after this house of wisdom was opened,
the vizier Abu l-Faraj carried off twenty-five camel loads of books
and sold them for 100,000 dinars to pay his soldiery. A few
months later the Turkish soldiers defeated the caliph's forces,
invaded the palace, and plundered it thoroughly. The military
mob tore the fine leather bindings off the books and made
shoes of them. The manuscript pages were either thrown in
heaps on the sand or burned in a place near Abyar, which long
afterward was known as the "Hill of the Books."[38] After this disaster, the Fatimid princes again began to collect books energeti-
cally; and when, a century later, in 1171, Saladin entered Cairo,
he found a library of 120,000 volumes in the palace. He gave
these books to his learned chancellor Al-Qadi al-Fadil.[39] . . .

When the Arabs conquered Spain in 711, they did not have to
contend with a deeply rooted homogeneous culture. The Visigoths, who had preceded the Arabs as invaders, were not greatly
given to learning. Byzantine influence was confined to the south;
Catholicism was limited to Latin; and the Jews had their own
academies, wherein were taught Hebrew and Aramaic.[45] Hence
the Muslims, who made Cordova their capital, had an almost un-
limited field in which to create their own culture.[46]

Spanish–Arabic civilization duplicated the patterns of Muslim
activities in Syria and Egypt. At Cordova, as in Bagdad and

[36] Al-Maqrizi, quoted in Pinto, op. cit., pp. 227–28.
[38] Lane-Poole, op. cit., p. 149.
[39] Ibid., p. 193.
[45] R. Altamira, A History of Spanish Civilization, tr. by P. Volkov (London,
1930), pp. 45, 47.
[46] The best guide to Arabic libraries and schools is J. Ribera y Tarragó, Diserta-
ciones y opusculos (Madrid, 1928), especially his "Bibliofilos y bibliotecas en la
España musulmana," I, 181–228, which was separately printed in Cordova (3rd ed.;
1925); also H. Derenbourgh, Les Manuscrits arabes de l'Escurial (Paris, 1929).

Cairo, the caliphs were scholars and patrons of letters. In Spain, as in the Near East and North Africa, the Arabs introduced new crops, improved agriculture, extended irrigation, built factories, founded rich cities, and raised the general prosperity of the land. Cordova became probably the largest city in Europe after Constantinople, possessing 200,000 houses, 600 mosques, and 900 public baths. The streets were stone-paved, and water was brought to the houses in conduits; public lighting illuminated the streets at night. The palace of the caliphs had 21 doors and was surrounded by 1,293 columns of marble and jasper with gilded capitals; it was illuminated by hundreds of silver lamps. To Christendom, Cordova was a marvelous, a fabulous city; and it attracted many amazed travelers from northern Spain, France, Italy, and even Germany.[47] . . .

Arabic Spain had no less than seventy libraries, established in all the important cities. The greatest library—no doubt the largest in the world at that time—was founded by Caliph Hakim II (d. 976) in Cordova. Hakim is reputed to have been of fabulous erudition, although the Arabic source on the subject is not above reproach. One Moslem historian writes:

> Not one book was to be found in Hakim's library, whatever might be its contents, which the Caliph had not perused, writing on the flyleaf the name, surname, and patronymic of the author; that of the tribe to which he belonged; the year of his birth and death.[49]

Whether this is true or not, there is no doubt that Hakim did not confine himself merely to reading, but gathered in Cordova distinguished men of letters and collected books on an extensive scale. He had agents in all the book marts of the Moslem world. Generous and lavish, Hakim not only supported poor scholars and students (he paid the teachers of his twenty-seven free schools in Cordova out of his own pocket), but once paid 1,000

[47] Altamira, op. cit., pp. 49–51; M. Casiri, *Biblioteca arabico-hispana escurialensis* (Madrid, 1760–70), II, 151.
[49] Ibn al-Abar, quoted by al-Makkari, *The History of Mohammedan Dynasties in Spain*, tr. by P. de Gayangos (London, 1843), II, 170.

dinars for the first copy of Abu al-Faraj's *Book of Songs.*[50] "Al-Hakim," the historian Ibn al-Abar relates, "was the most virtuous and liberal of men; and he treated all those who came to his court with the utmost kindness."[51]

The library finally contained from 400,000 to 600,000 volumes, some of which are supposed to have been catalogued and annotated by the caliph himself. To quote Ibn al-Abar once more:

> I was told by Talid, the eunuch, who was the keeper of the library and repository of the sciences in the palace of the Beni Merwan, that the catalogue only of the books consisted of forty-four volumes, each volume having twenty sheets of paper, which contained nothing but the titles and descriptions of the books.[52]

A staff of librarians, copyists, and binders was housed in the scriptorium of the palace of Merwan, where the collection was housed. . . .

The birth of science in the West is perhaps the most glorious part of the history of Muslim libraries, as it was certainly the last chapter of importance. In order to understand this subject it is necessary to remember that Spain was conquered by the Muslimized Moors in 711 and converted into the caliphate of Cordova, and that Sicily was a Muslim province from 831 to 1090, while the close proximity of the great island to southern Italy subjected the "toe of the boot" to a heavy Muslim influence. Accordingly, it was through Lower Italy and Spain that Muslim science—which it must be remembered was remotely of Greek, Persian, or Hindu origin—penetrated into western Europe.

The first gateway was southern Italy. The beginning of the medical school at Salerno seems to be remotely referable to Byzantine influence, but it was influenced in the tenth century by Arabian medicine through Shabbethai ben-Abraham ben-Joel, a

---

[50] Al-Makkari, *op. cit.*, p. 168; Nicholson, *op. cit.*, p. 419.

[51] Ibn al-Abar, quoted in al-Makkari, *op. cit.*, pp. 168–169.

[52] Ibn al-Abar being the only source on the subject, it is necessary to caution the reader that he was writing in 1210, about two and a quarter centuries after the time of Hakim.

Jew of Otranto in Lower Italy, who was taken captive by Saracen pirates in 925 and carried to Palermo, where he learned Arabic and "studied all the sciences of the Greeks, the Arabs, the Babylonians and Hindus." Southern Italy at this time, it must be remembered, was a Byzantine possession; and Sicily had been conquered by the Mohammedans in the ninth century. Accordingly, Greek and Arabic learning met in the schools of Salerno, Otranto, Rossano, and Monte Cassino. In 950 John, of the monastery of Gorze in Lorraine, brought to Germany from Calabria copies of Aristotle's *Categories* and Porphyry's *Isagoge*.

This same John of Gorze was also the earliest instrument for the conveyance of Arabic science north of the Alps and the earliest agent of its dissemination in Europe. In 953 the German emperor Otto the Great sent John of Gorze on a diplomatic mission to the caliph Abd-er-Rahman III of Cordova, where John fell in with the distinguished Spanish-Jewish scholar Ibn Shaprut, who stood high in the favor of the caliph. John was gone nearly three years and in that time learned the Arabic language. When he returned to Germany in 956, he brought back with him a horseload of Arabic books. We are not told definitely what these were. But constructive evidence shows that some of them must have been of a scientific nature, for in the eleventh century there was a remarkable outflowering of interest in science, especially in mathematics, in the schools of Lorraine, whence the interest extended down the Rhine into Flanders.[57] There is reason to believe that at least some slight interest in Arabic science must have been cultivated in the Lotharingian and Flemish schools, for, when Knut the Danish king conquered England (1000–1035), he distrusted the native Anglo-Saxon bishops and imported Lotharingian and Flemish churchmen in that capacity, five of whom had some knowledge of Arabian science. The most notable of these was Robert de Losinga, bishop of Hereford, a place which in the late twelfth century was an active center of Arabic studies in England. In the same century Guibert de Nogent, a French abbot who died in 1124, was the

[57] J. W. Thompson, "The Introduction of Arabic Science into Lorraine in the Tenth Century," *Isis*, XII (1929), 184–94.

author of a remarkable tribute to the value of Arabic astronomy.[58] . . .

By 1200, in addition to works on optics and physics and per-
spective in general, the whole corpus of Greek medicine—the
works of Hippocrates and Galen—were available in Latin translations, together with a comprehensive summary of Arabic medicine in Avicenna's *Canon of Medicine.* Just as the early Middle
Ages had had to digest such science as was contained in Pliny's
Natural History and Seneca's *Natural Questions* and other ancient Roman writers, so the later Middle Ages had now to digest
and to understand the new Greek-Arabic learning. With large
omissions, of course, western Europe by the thirteenth century
had inherited the legacy of four great cultures—Greek, Greco-
oriental, Byzantine, and Arabic.[65] . . .

To conclude: Before the middle of the thirteenth century the
most valuable material in Islamic libraries had been acquired
by European scholarship in the form of translation. It was just
in time. As we have already seen, the Mohammedan East was
nearly destroyed by the invasions of the Mongols in the middle
of the thirteenth century and did not begin to recover until the
rise of the Ottoman Turks in the fifteenth century. In the West
a longer duration to Islam was granted. The expulsion of the
Moors from Spain in 1492 was followed by a holocaust of thousands of Arabic books. What books were saved found lodgment
in libraries in Fez or Tunis. In the sack of Tunis in 1536 by the
emperor Charles V, all books written in Arabic were burned.
Spain was so stripped of Arabic manuscripts that, when Philip II
founded the Escorial, no Arabic manuscripts could be found in
the kingdom. Fortunately, the capture of a Moroccan galley in
which a considerable number of Arabic books and manuscripts
was found relieved the royal librarian's embarrassment. But in
June, 1674, fire broke out in the Escorial and destroyed 8,000
Arabic books. A century later, when Michael Casiri began to
catalogue the Arabic collection in the Escorial, he found only

---

[58] *Ibid.,* p. 191 and n. 33.
[65] Sibyl D. Wingate, *The Medieval Latin Version of the Aristotelian Scientific
Corpus, with Special Reference to the Biological Works* (London, 1931).

1,824 manuscripts—forlorn survivors, perhaps, of the once great libraries of Cordova.

MONASTIC LIBRARIES

Early Middle Ages

Devout men under highly developed religions everywhere have tried to achieve better lives through pursuing paths different and apart from those followed by their contemporaries. Many a staunch believer has become a hermit (eremitical monasticism) or has joined a community of like-minded men who make similar vows of chastity, poverty, and obedience to a prescribed rule (cenobitical monasticism).

Christian monasticism began in the early fourth century in central Egypt, when St. Anthony the Great undertook to instruct other hermits who dwelled near his cell and desired to emulate his asceticism. Fifteen years later, St. Pachomius brought into a self-supporting monastery a group of monks who were assigned specific tasks, although their daily lives were not strictly regulated—for instance, a monk could choose to eat his meals alone or with others. Late in the fourth century, St. Basil the Great, who had observed monasticism in Egypt, required his monks to meet for prayers and meals at set times, and, following his lead, monasticism under a rule was established in Greece and in Slavic countries. St. Athanasius, a fugitive from Alexandria, helped to establish, in 340, a cenobitical mode of living for the cathedral clergy in northern Italy. But not until the early sixth century, when St. Benedict developed his Holy Rule for the monks on Monte Cassino, did Western monasteries have a common code for the regulation of the lives of the monks. Within the next two centuries, all of the monasteries in Western Europe, with the exception of those in Ireland and a few in Spain, adopted St. Benedict's practical guide to sanctity through an ordered life in a religious community.

Italy

Although the purpose of monasticism is to improve the spiritual life and understanding of the participants, the need in Christian monasteries for the capacity to read the Scriptures and other religious works soon led to the copying of manuscripts and to the teaching of the

Latin language. St. Pachomius's rule prescribed lessons in reading and writing thrice daily, and books in his monastery were kept in a cupboard from which a volume could be borrowed by a brother for one week. According to one of St. Augustine's letters, the nuns at Hippo in North Africa had a library from which books were obtained at the hours set for reading. The classic statement of the role of reading in monasteries is to be found in St. Benedict's Rule:

> Idleness is the enemy of the soul; hence brethren ought, at certain hours, to occupy themselves with manual labor, and at other hours in sacred reading. . . .
>
> From Easter until September 14 let them apply themselves to reading from the fourth hour until about the sixth. . . . From September the 14th to the beginning of Lent, let them apply themselves to reading until the end of the second hour. . . .
>
> During Lent let them apply themselves to reading from morning until the end of the third hour. . . . In these days of Lent let them each receive a book from the library, and read it straight through. These books are to be given out at the beginning of Lent. One or two senior monks should go round the monastery at the times set for reading, to see that there be no slothful brother who spends his time in idleness or gossip and neglects his reading, so that he not only harms himself but also disturbs others.

The Order of Cluny, founded in 912, introduced another corrective:

> On the second day of Lent the only passage of the Rule to be read is that concerning the observance of Lent.
>
> Then shall be read aloud a record of the books which a year before had been given out to brethren for their reading. When a brother's name is called, he rises, and returns the book that had been given to him; and if it should happen that he has not read it through, he is to ask forgiveness for his lack of diligence.
>
> A carpet on which those books are to be laid out is to be put down in the Chapter-House; and the titles of those which are distributed anew to the brethren are to be noted on a tablet for this purpose.

Although the Benedictine monasteries were more concerned with the ill effects of idleness than with the merits of reading, the literary labors of the monks at Vivarium, under Cassiodorus, were of a different nature. During the first half of the sixth century, Flavius Magnus Aurelius Cassiodorus Senator had occupied high posts in the Gothic court at Ravenna, but the overthrow of the Visigoths by the Byzantines caused him to leave politics for religion and to establish a religious community on his ancestral estate on the southern coast of Italy. Cassiodorus perceived the need for education among his monks, and he wrote a number of books for their instruction and set down rules to be followed in copying manuscripts. Several of his works were exceedingly popular in monasteries during succeeding centuries of the Middle Ages. Especially favored was the Institutiones—in two parts— one of which deals with interpretation of the Bible and study of the Fathers, and the other with liberal arts. Leslie W. Jones, in his article on "The Influence of Cassiodorus on Mediaeval Culture," wrote that Cassiodorus was the first "to make of the monastery a theological school and a scriptorium for the multiplication of copies of the Scripture, of the Fathers of the Church and the commentators, and of the great secular writers of antiquity."[11] According to Professor A. D. Momigliano of the University of London, Cassiodorus's belief that classical scholarship could contribute to monastic life was important in the development of medieval civilization.

Cassiodorus lived on in the monastery at Vivarium until he was past ninety. His labors there among his monks are reviewed and evaluated by Thomas Hodgkin in his introduction to The Letters of Cassiodorus (London: Henry Frowde, 1886), pp. 54–60:

It can have surprised none of the friends of Cassiodorus when the veteran statesman announced his intention of spending the remainder of his days in monastic retirement. He was now sixty years of age; his wife, if he had ever married, was probably by this time dead; and we hear nothing of any children for whose sake he need have remained longer in the world. The Emperor would probably have received him gladly into his service, but

[11] Leslie W. Jones, "The Influence of Cassiodorus on Mediaeval Culture," Speculum, October 1945, p. 434.

Cassiodorus had now done with politics. The dream of his life had been to build up an independent Italian State, strong with the strength of the Goths, and wise with the wisdom of the Romans. That dream was now scattered to the winds. Providence had made it plain that not by this bridge was civilisation to pass over from the Old World to the New. Cassiodorus accepted the decision, and consecrated his old age to religious meditation and to a work even more important than any of his political labours (though one which must be lightly touched on here), the preservation by the pens of monastic copyists of the Christian Scriptures, and of the great works of classical antiquity.

It was to his ancestral Scyllacium that Cassiodorus retired; and here, between the mountains of Aspromonte and the sea, he founded his monastery, or, more accurately, his two monasteries, one for the austere hermit, and the other for the less aspiring coenobite. The former was situated among the "sweet recesses of Mons Castellius," the latter among the well-watered gardens which took their name from the Vivaria (fish-ponds) that Cassiodorus had constructed among them in connection with the river Pellena. Baths, too, especially intended for the use of the sick, had been prepared on the banks of the stream. Here in monastic simplicity, but not without comfort, Cassiodorus ordained that his monks should dwell. The Rule of the order—in so far as it had a written Rule—was drawn from the writings of Cassian, the great founder of Western Monachism, who had died about a century before the Vivarian monastery was founded. In commending the writings of Cassian to the study of his monks, Cassiodorus warns them against the bias shown in them towards the Semi–Pelagian heresy, and desires them to choose the good in those treatises and to refuse the evil. Whatever the reason may have been, it seems clear that Cassiodorus did not make the Rule of Benedict the law of his new monastery; and indeed, strange as the omission may appear, there is, I believe, no allusion to that great contemporary Saint, the "Father of Monks," in the whole of his writings.

Though the founder and patron of these two monasteries, it seems probable that Cassiodorus never formally assumed the office of Abbot in either of them. He had probably still some duties to perform as a large landholder in Bruttii; but besides these he had also work to do for "his monks" (as he affectionately called them)—work of a literary and educational kind— which perhaps made it undesirable that he should be burdened with the petty daily routine of an Abbot's duties. Some years before, he had endeavoured to induce Pope Agapetus to found a School of Theology and Christian Literature at Rome, in imitation of the schools of Alexandria and Nisibis. The clash of arms consequent on the invasion of Italy by Belisarius had prevented the fulfilment of this scheme; but the aged statesman now determined to devote the remainder of his days to the accomplishment of the same purpose in connection with the Vivarian convent.

In the earliest days of Monasticism men like the hermits of the Thebaid had thought of little else but mortifying the flesh by vigils and fastings, and withdrawing from all human voices to enjoy an ecstatic communion with their Maker. The life in common of monks like those of Nitria and Lerinum had chastened some of the extravagances of these lonely enthusiasts while still keeping their main ends in view. St. Jerome, in his cell at Bethlehem, had shown what great results might be obtained for the Church of all ages from the patient literary toil of one religious recluse. And finally St. Benedict, in that Rule of his which was to be the code of monastic Christendom for centuries, had sanctified Work as one of the most effectual preservatives of the bodily and spiritual health of the ascetic, bringing together *Laborare* and *Orare* in friendly union, and proclaiming anew for the monk as for the untonsured citizen the primal ordinance, "In the sweat of thy brow thou shalt eat bread."

The great merit of Cassiodorus, that which shows his deep insight into the needs of his age and entitles him to the eternal gratitude of Europe, was his determination to utilise the vast leisure of the convent for the preservation of Divine and human learning and for its transmission to after ages. In the miserable circumstances of the times Theology was in danger of becoming brutified and ignorant; the great treasures of Pagan literature were no longer being perpetuated by the slaves who had once acted as *librarii* to the Greek or Roman noble; and with every movement of the Ostrogothic armies, or of the yet more savage hordes who served under the Imperial standard, with every sacked city and with every ravaged villa, some Codex, it may be such as we should now deem priceless and irreplaceable, was perishing. This being the state of Italy, Cassiodorus resolved to make of his monastery not merely a place for pious meditation, but a theological school and a manufactory for the multiplication of copies, not only of the Scriptures, not only of the Fathers and the commentators on Scripture, but also of the great writers of pagan antiquity. In the chapter which he devotes to the description of the *scriptorium* of his monastery he describes, with an enthusiasm which must have been contagious, the noble work done there by the *antiquarius*: "He may fill his mind with the Scriptures while copying the sayings of the Lord. With his fingers he gives life to men and arms them against the wiles of the devil. So many wounds does Satan receive as the *antiquarius* copies words of Christ. What he writes in his cell will be scattered far and wide over distant Provinces. Man multiplies the heavenly words, and by a striking figure—if I may dare so to speak —the three fingers of his hand express the utterances of the Holy Trinity. The fast-travelling reed writes down the holy words, and thus avenges the malice of the Wicked One, who caused a reed to be used to smite the head of the Saviour."

It is true that the passage here quoted refers only to the work of the copyist of the Christian Scriptures, but it could easily be shown from other passages that the literary activity of the monastery was not confined to these, but was also employed on secular literature.

Cassiodorus then goes on to describe the care which he has taken for the binding of the sacred Codices in covers worthy of the beauty of their contents, following the example of the householder in the parable, who provided wedding garments for all who came to the supper of his son. One pattern volume had been prepared, containing samples of various sorts of binding, that the amanuensis might choose that which pleased him best. He had moreover provided, to help the nightly toil of the *scriptorium*, mechanical lamps of some wonderful construction, which appears to have made them self-trimming, and to have ensured their having always a sufficient supply of oil. Sun-dials also for bright days, and water-clocks for cloudy days and the night-season, regulated their labour, and admonished them when it was time to unclose the three fingers, to lay down the reed, and to assemble with their brethren in the chapel of the convent for psalmody and prayer.

Upon the whole, though the idea of using the convent as a place of literary toil and theological training was not absolutely new, Cassiodorus seems certainly entitled to the praise of having first realised it systematically and on an extensive scale. It was entirely in harmony with the spirit of the Rule of St. Benedict, if it was not formally ordained in that document. At a very early date in the history of their order, the Benedictines, influenced probably by the example of the monastery of Vivaria, commenced that long series of services to the cause of literature which they have never wholly intermitted. Thus, instead of accepting the obsolete formula for which some scholars in the last age contended, "Cassiodorus was a Benedictine," we should perhaps be rather justified in maintaining that Benedict, or at least his immediate followers, were Cassiodorians.

In order to set an example of literary diligence to his monks, and to be able to sympathise with the difficulties of an amanuensis, Cassiodorus himself transcribed the Psalter, the Prophets, and the Epistles, no doubt from the translation of Jerome. This is not the place for enlarging on the merits of Cassiodorus as a custodian and transmitter of the sacred text. They were no doubt considerable; and the rules which he gives to his monks, to guide them in the work of transcription, show that he belonged to the Conservative school of critics, and was anxious to guard against hasty emendations of the text, however plausible. Practically, however, his MSS. of the Latin Scriptures, showing the Itala and the Vulgate in parallel columns, seem to have been answerable for some of that confusion between the two versions which to some extent spoiled the text of Jerome, without preserving to us in its purity the interesting translation of the earlier Church.

Besides his labours as a transcriber, Cassiodorus, both as an original author and a compiler, used his pen for the instruction of his fellow-inmates at Vivarium.

Ireland

During the sixth century, when the monasteries led by St. Benedict and Cassiodorus were being founded in Italy, books and learning had a congenial home in Ireland. The origins of the high level of culture attributed to Irish monasteries in the fifth and sixth centuries are obscure, but in the seventh century the island did furnish books and teachers to England and the Continent. One outstanding authority, Montague Rhodes James, observed in The Wanderings and Homes of Manuscripts, that the Irish learning of the late fifth and sixth centuries began with the influx of teachers from France, who had fled before the barbarian invasions in the fifth century,[12] but he did not develop this provocative suggestion. An enthusiastic view of The Irish Element in Mediæval Culture is given in a small volume by a nineteenth century German scholar, H. Zimmer. According to this account, in the third and fourth centuries British missionaries preached among the Celtic tribes; hence, Christian learning in Ireland "derived without interruption" from the Church Fathers Ambrose, Jerome, and Augustine. "Here also were to be found such specimens of classical literature as Virgil's works . . . and an acquaintance with Greek authors as well."[13] But well-supported tradition maintains that St. Palladius and St. Patrick went to Ireland in the fifth century, and that their work (in particular St. Patrick's) led to the introduction of the Latin language and the establishment of schools for the education of priests at Armagh, Bangor, and elsewhere.

St. Patrick's missionary work of the fifth century was extended in the sixth and early seventh centuries by two Irish monks, St. Columba, who founded a famous monastery school on the island of Iona off the west coast of Scotland, and St. Columban, who helped to establish monasteries on the Continent, which were distinguished for their libraries at Luxeuil, Bobbio, and St. Gall. Their work, and that of other learned Irish monks in the seventh century, is related in Ern-

---

[12] Montague Rhodes James, The Wanderings and Homes of Manuscripts (London: Society for Promoting Christian Knowledge, 1919), p. 25.

[13] H. Zimmer, The Irish Element in Mediæval Culture, trans. by Jane Loring Edmands (New York: Putnam, 1891), p. 19.

est A. *Savage's* Old English Libraries (*London: Methuen, 1911*), pp. 3–9:

> St. Patrick received his sacred education at Marmoutier; under Germanus at Auxerre; and possibly at Lérins. His companions on his mission to Ireland, and the missionaries who followed him, nearly all came from the same centres. Naturally, therefore, the same practices would be observed, not only in regard to religious discipline and organisation, but in regard to instruction and study. Even the mysterious Palladius, Patrick's forerunner, is said to have left books in Ireland. But the earliest important references to that use of books which distinguishes the educated missionary from the mere fanatical recluse are in connexion with Patrick. Pope Sixtus is said to have given him books in plenty to take with him to Ireland. Later he is supposed to have visited Rome, whence he brought books home to Armagh. He gave copies of parts of the Scriptures to Irish chieftains. To one Fiacc he gave a case containing a bell, a crosier, tablets, and a meinister, which, according to Dr. Lanigan, may have been a cumdach enclosing the Gospels and the vessels for the sacred ministry, or, according to Dr. Whitley Stokes, simply a credence-table. He sometimes gave a missal (*lebar nuird*). He had books at Tara. On one occasion his books were dropped into the water and were "drowned." Presumably the books he distributed came from the Gallic schools, although his followers no doubt began transcribing as opportunity offered and as material came to hand. Patrick himself wrote alphabets, sometimes called the "elements"; most likely the elements or the A B C of the Christian doctrine, corresponding with the "primer."
>
> This was the dawn of letters for Ireland. By disseminating the Scriptures and these primers, Patrick and his followers, and the train of missionaries who came afterwards, secured the knowledge and use of the Roman alphabet. The way was clear for the free introduction of schools and books and learning. "St. Patrick did not do for the Scots what Wulfilas did for the Goths, and the Slavonic apostles for the Slavs; he did not translate the sacred books of his religion into Irish and found a national church literature. . . . What Patrick, on the other hand, and his fellow-

workers did was to diffuse a knowledge of Latin in Ireland. To the circumstance that he adopted this line of policy, and did not attempt to create a national ecclesiastical language, must be ascribed the rise of the schools of learning which distinguished Ireland in the sixth and seventh centuries."

Mainly owing to the labours of Dr. John Healy, we now know a good deal about the somewhat slow growth of the Irish schools to fame; but for our purpose it will do to learn something of them in their heyday, when at last we hear certainly of that free use of books which must have been common for some time. From the sixth to the eighth century Ireland enjoyed an eminent place in the world of learning; and the lives and works of her scholars imply book-culture of good character. St. Columba was famed for his studious occupations. Educated first by Finnian of Moville, then by another tutor of the same name at the famous school of Clonard, he journeyed to other centres for further instruction after his ordination. From youth he loved books and studies. He is represented as reading out of doors at the moment when the murderer of a young girl is struck dead. In later life he realized the importance of monastic records. He had annals compiled, and bards preserved and arranged them in the monastic chests. At Iona the brethren of his settlement passed their time in reading and transcribing, as well as in manual labour. Very careful were they to copy correctly. Baithen, a monk on Iona, got one of his fellows to look over a Psalter which he had just finished writing, but only a single error was discovered. Columba himself became proficient in copying and illuminating. He could not spend an hour without study, or prayer, or writing, or some other holy occupation. He transcribed, we are told, over three hundred copies of the Gospels or the Psalter—a magnification of a saint's powers by a devout biographer, but significant as it testifies to Columba's love of studious labours, and shows how highly these ascetics thought of work of this kind. On two occasions, being a man as well as a saint, he broke into violence when crossed in his love of books. One story tells how he visited a holy and learned recluse named Longarad, whose much-prized books he wished to see. Being denied, he became wroth and cursed Longarad. "May the books be of no use to you," he cried, "nor to any one after you, since you withhold them." So far the tale is not improbable, but a little embroidery completes a legend. The books became unintelligible, so the story continues, the moment Longarad died. At the same instant the satchels in all the Irish schools and in Columba's cell slipped off their hooks on to the ground.

A quarrel about a book, we are told, changed his career. He borrowed a Psalter from Finnian of Moville, and made a copy of it, working secretly at night. Finnian heard of the piracy, and, as owner of the original, claimed the copy. Columba refused to let him have it. Then Diarmid, King of Meath, was asked to arbitrate. Arguing that as every calf belonged to its cow, so every copy of a book belonged to the owner of the original, he decided in Finnian's favour. Columba thought the award unjust, and said so. A little later, after another dispute with Diarmid on a question of monastic immunity, he called together his tribesmen and partisans, and offered battle. Diarmid was defeated. For some reason, not quite clear, these quarrels led to Columba's voluntary exile (c. 563). He sailed from Ireland, and landed upon the silver strand of Iona, and to the end of his days his work lay almost entirely amid the heather-covered uplands and plains of this little island home. Iona became a renowned centre of missionary work, quite overshadowing in importance the earlier "Scottish" settlement of Whitherne or Candida Casa. Pilgrims went thither from Ireland and England to receive instruction, and returned to carry on pioneer work in their own homeland. Thence went forth missionaries to carry the Christian message throughout Scotland and northern England. Perhaps, too, here was planned the expedition to far-off Iceland. "Before Iceland was peopled by the Northmen there were in the country those men whom the Northmen called Papar. They were Christian men, and the people believed that they came from the West, because Irish books and bells and crosiers were found after them, and still more things by which one might know that they were west-men, i.e., Irish."

Not only to the far north, but to the Continent, did the Irish

press their energetic way. In Gaul their chief missionary was
Columban (c. 543–615), who had been educated at Bangor,
then famous for the learning of its brethren. His works display an
extensive acquaintance with Christian and Latin literature. Both
the Greek and Hebrew languages may have been known to him,
though this seems improbable and inconceivable. In his Rule he
provides for teaching in schools, copying manuscripts, and for
daily reading.

The monasteries of Luxeuil, Bobio, and St. Gall, founded by
him and his companions on their mission in Gaul and Italy, became the homes of the most famous conventual libraries in the
world—a result surely traceable to the example set by the Irish
ascetics, and to the tradition they established.

Other Irish monks are better known for their literary attainments than for missionary enterprise. St. Cummian, in a letter
written about 634, displays much knowledge of theological literature, and a good deal of knowledge of a general kind. Another
monk named Augustine (c. 650) quotes from Eusebius and
Jerome in a work affording many other evidences of learning.
Aileran (c. 660), abbot of Clonard, wrote a religious work which
proves his acquaintance with Jerome, Philo, Cassian, Origen, and
Augustine.

An Englishman supplies valuable evidence of the state of Irish
learning. Aldhelm's (c. 656–709) works prove him to have had
access in England to a good library; while in one learned letter
he compares English schools favourably with the Irish, and declares Theodore and Hadrian would put Irish scholars in the
shade. Yet he is on his mettle when communicating with Irish
friends or pupils; he clearly reserves for them the flowers of his
eloquence. The Irish schools were indeed successful rivals of
the English schools, and Irish scholars could use libraries as good,
or nearly as good, as that at Aldhelm's disposal. At this time
the attraction which Ireland and Iona had for English students
was extraordinary. English crowded the Irish schools, although
the Canterbury school was not full. The city of Armagh was divided into three sections, one being called Trian-Saxon, the
Saxon's third, from the great number of Saxon students living
there.

In 664 many English, both high and low in rank, left their native land for Ireland, where they sought instruction in sacred studies, or an opportunity to lead a more ascetic life. Some devoted themselves faithfully to a monkish career. Others applied themselves to study only, and for that purpose journeyed from one master's cell to another. The Irish welcomed all comers. All received without charge daily food: barley or oaten bread and water, or sometimes milk—*cibus sit vilis et vespertinus*—a plain meal, once a day, in the afternoon. Books were supplied, or what is more likely, waxed tablets folded in book form. Teaching was as free as the open air in which it was carried on.

Among the English at one time or another taking advantage of Irish hospitality were Gildas (c. 540), first native historian of England; Ecgberht, presbyter, a Northumbrian of noble birth; Ethelhun, brother of Ethelwin, bishop of Lindsay; Oswald, king of Northumbria; Aldfrith, another Northumbrian king, who was educated either in Ireland or Iona; Alcuin, who received instruction at Clonmacnoise; one named Wictberht, "notable . . . for his learning and knowledge, for he had lived many years as a stranger and pilgrim in Ireland"; and St. Willibrord, who at the age of twenty journeyed to Ireland for purposes of study, because he had heard that learning flourished in that country.

Northumbria and York

The conversion of the English began in 595 with the mission of forty monks, headed by St. Augustine, which was sent by Pope Gregory from Rome. Augustine founded a monastery at Canterbury, made thousands of converts in southeast England, and strove, before his death in 604, to reconcile the Celtic bishops to the Roman Catholic Church.

Late in the seventh century, Benedict Biscop, a Northumbrian, made two pilgrimages to Rome before becoming a monk at Lérins. He later made three more trips to Rome during each of which he collected books and relics which he carried to Britain for use and display in the monasteries he established at Wearmouth (674) and at nearby Jarrow in Northumbria. On his last trip, Benedict Biscop brought from Rome a chanter from St. Peter's and a Benedictine abbot who instructed the Northumbrian monks in the music and liturgy of the Church at Rome.

The Venerable Bede, who was born about 673 in Northumbria, spent his life in the religious houses at Wearmouth and Jarrow. Most of his sixty-odd years were devoted to meditation and study of the books in the library formed mainly by Benedict Biscop. Many of Bede's own writings, including his Historia Ecclesiastica Gentis Anglorum, were written for the instruction of monks in Northumbria, but his influence reached to the Continent and led to the establishment of the cathedral school at York, which became famous under Alcuin before he left in 782 to head the palace school at the court of Charlemagne.

St. Boniface, a Devonshire monk, served for thirty-five years as a missionary in Germany, where he helped to form monasteries at Fulda and elsewhere. Boniface wrote repeatedly to England for books, including one of Bede's, which he described as "a spark from the candle of the church, lighted by the Holy Spirit in your northern land." He sought and obtained books from Egbert, archbishop of York, and he implored a former student to "take pity upon an old man, worn out by the storms of the German sea," and to send "whatever you may find in your church library which you think would be useful to me and which I may not be aware of or may not have in written form."

Wilhelm Levison, a close student of the intellectual relations between England and the Continent in the Eighth Century, points out that while the Anglo-Saxons brought many manuscripts to France and Germany, even more important was their pride in the possession of beautiful books and the sense of their utility which instilled new vigor into the cultural activity fostered by Charlemagne.[14] The literary culture which flowered during the eighth century in England, especially in Northumbria and at York, is reviewed in a second selection from Ernest A. Savage's Old English Libraries (London: Methuen, 1911), pp. 30–36:

> Meanwhile Northumbria had become one of the leading centres of learning in Europe, almost entirely through the labours and

[14] Wilhelm Levison, England and the Continent in the Eighth Century (Oxford: Clarendon Press, 1946), p. 147.

influence of Irish missionaries. St. Aidan, an ascetic of Iona who journeyed to Northumbria at King Oswald's request, founded Lindisfarne, which became the monastic and episcopal capital of that kingdom. Aidan required all his pupils, whether religious or laymen, to read the Scriptures, or to learn the Psalms. The education of boys was a part of his system. Wherever a monastery was founded it became a school wherein taught the monks who had followed him from Scotland. Cedd, the founder and abbot of Lastingham, was Aidan's pupil, so was his brother, the great bishop Ceadda (Chad), who succeeded him in his abbacy. At Lindisfarne was wrought by Eadfrith (d. 721) the beautiful manuscript of the Gospels now preserved in the British Museum, and a little later the fine cover for it. Lastingham, founded on the desolate moorland of North Yorkshire, "among steep and distant mountains, which looked more like lurking-places for robbers and dens of wild beasts, than dwellings of men," upheld the traditions of the Columban houses for piety, asceticism, and studious occupations. Thither repaired one Owini, not to live idle, but to labour, and as he was less capable of studying, he applied himself earnestly to manual work, the while better-instructed monks were indoors reading.

In many directions do we observe traces of Aidan's good work. Hild, the foundress of Whitby Abbey, was for a short time his pupil. Her monastery was famous for having educated five bishops, among them John of Beverley, and for giving birth, in Caedmon, to the father of English poetry. "Religious poetry, sung to the harp as it passed from hand to hand, must have flourished in the monastery of the abbess Hild, and the kernel of Bede's story concerning the birth of our earliest poet must be that the brethren and sisters on that bleak northern shore spoke 'to each other in psalms and hymns and spiritual songs.'" Of Melrose, an offshoot of Aidan's foundation, the sainted Cuthbert was an inmate. At Lindisfarne, where "he speedily learned the Psalms and some other books," the great Wilfrid was a novice. Of his studies, indeed, we know little: he seems to have sought prelatical power rather than learning. But he and his followers were responsible for the conversion of the Northumbrian church from Columban to Roman usages, and the introduction of Benedictinism into the monasteries; and consequently, for bringing the studies of the monks into line with the rules of Benedict's order.

Such progress would have been impossible had not the rulers of Northumbria from Oswald to Aldfrith been friendly to Christianity. Aldfrith had been educated at Iona, and was a man of studious disposition. His predecessor had advanced Northumbria's reputation enormously by giving Benedict Biscop (629–90) sites for his monasteries of Wearmouth and Jarrow. We know enough of this Benedict to wish we knew very much more. He suggests to us enthusiasm for his cause, and energy and foresight in labouring for it. Naturally, Aldhelm's writings have gained him far more attention in literary histories than the Northumbrian has received. But the influence of Benedict, a man of much learning, wide-travelled, was at least as great and as far-reaching. Lérins, the great centre of monachism in Gaul, and Canterbury under Theodore, had been his schools. On six occasions he flitted back and forth to Rome, and to go to Rome, in those days, was a liberal education, both in worldly and spiritual affairs. Not a little of his influence was the direct outcome of his book-collecting. From all his journeys to Rome he is said to have returned laden with books. He certainly came back from his fourth journey with a great number of books of all kinds. He also obtained books at Vienne. His sixth and last journey to Rome was wholly devoted to collecting books, classical as well as theological. When he died he left instructions for the preservation of the most noble and rich library he had gathered together. "If we consider how difficult, fatiguing, . . . even dangerous a journey between the British Islands and Italy must have been in those days of anarchy and barbarism, we can appreciate the intensity of Benedict's passion for beautiful and costly volumes." The library he formed was worthy of the labour, we cannot doubt: possibly was the best then in Britain. It served as the model for the still more famous collection at York. The scholarship of Bede, who used it in writing his works, proclaims its value for literary purposes. Bede tells us he always applied himself to Scriptural study, and in the intervals of observing monastic discipline and singing daily in the church, he took pleasure in learning, or teaching, or writing. The picture of Bede in his solitary monastery, leading a placid life among Benedict's books, poring over the beautifully-wrought pages with the scholar's tense calm to find the material in the Fathers and the historians, and to seek the apt quotation from the classics, must always flash to the mind at the mere mention of his name. Every fact in connexion with his work testifies to the excellent equipment of his monastery for writing ecclesiastical history, and to the cordial way in which the religious co-operated for the advancement of learning and research.

Canterbury, Malmesbury, Lindisfarne, Wearmouth and Jarrow, and York were like mountain-peaks tipped with gold by the first rays of the rising sun, while all below remains dark. Yet while not indicative of widespread means of instruction, the existence of these centres, and the character of the work done in them, suggests that at other places the same sort of work, on a smaller and less influential scale, soon began. At Lichfield, on the moorland at Ripon, in "the dwelling-place in the meadows" at Peterborough, in the desolate fenland at Crowland and at Ely, on the banks of the Thames at Abingdon, and of the Avon at Evesham, in the nunneries of Barking and Wimborne, at Chertsey, Glastonbury, Gloucester, in the far north at Melrose, and even perhaps at Coldingham, Christianity was speeding its message, and learning—such as it was, primitive and pretentious —caught pale reflections from more famous places. Now and again definite facts are met with hinting at a spreading enlightenment. Acca, abbot and bishop of Hexham, for example "gave all diligence, as he does to this day," wrote Bede, "to procure relics of the blessed Apostles and martyrs of Christ. . . . Besides which, he industriously gathered the histories of their martyrdom, together with other ecclesiastical writings, and erected there a large and noble library." Of this library, unfortunately, there is not a wrack left behind. A tiny school was carried on at a monastery near Exeter, where Boniface was first instructed. At the monastery of Nursling he was taught grammar, history, poetry,

Plate IV The Venerable Bede

rhetoric, and the Scriptures; there also manuscripts were copied. Books were produced under Abbess Eadburh of Minster, a learned woman who corresponded with Boniface and taught the metric art. Boniface's letters throw interesting light on our subject. Eadburh sent him books, money, and other gifts. He also wrote home asking his old friend Bishop Daniel of Winchester for a fine manuscript of the six major prophets, which had been written in a large and clear hand by Winbert: no such book, he explains, can be had abroad, and his eyes are no longer strong enough to read with ease the small character of ordinary manuscripts. In another letter written to Ecgberht of York is recorded an exchange of books, and a request for a copy of the commentaries of Bede.

A decree of the Council held at Cloveshoe in 747, pointing out the want of instruction among the religious, and ordering all bishops, abbots, and abbesses to promote and encourage learning, whether it means that monkish education was on the wane or that it was not making such quick progress as was desired, at any rate does not mean that England was in a bad way in this respect, or that she lagged behind the Continent. On the contrary, England and Ireland were renowned homes of learning in Western Europe. Perhaps a few centres on the mainland could show libraries as good as those here; but certainly no country had such scholars. England's pre-eminence was recognized by Charles the Great when he invited Alcuin to his court (781).

Alcuin was brought up at York from childhood. In company with Albert, who taught the arts and grammar at this northern school, Alcuin visited Gaul and Rome to scrape together a few more books. On returning later he was entrusted with the care of the library: a task for which he was well fitted, if enthusiasm, breaking into rime, be a qualification:—

> "Small is the space which contains the gifts of heavenly Wisdom
> Which you, reader, rejoice piously here to receive;
> Better than richest gifts of the Kings, this treasure of Wisdom,

Light, for the seeker of this, shines on the road to the
Day."

York could not retain Alcuin long. Fortunately, just when dissensions among the English kings, and the Danish raids began to
harass England, and to threaten the coming decline of her learning, he was invited to take charge of a school established by
Charles the Great. Charles had undertaken the task of reviving
literary study, well-nigh extinguished through the neglect of his
ancestors; and he bade all his subjects to cultivate the arts. As far
as he could he accomplished the task, principally owing to the
aid of the English scholar and of willing helpers from Ireland.

Alcuin was soon at the head of St. Martin's of Tours where he
was responsible for the great activity of the scribes in his day. He
persuaded Charles to send a number of copyists to York. "I, your
Flavius," he writes, "according to your exhortation and wise
desire, have been busy under the roof of St. Martin, in dispens-
ing to some the honey of the Holy Scriptures. Others I strive to
inebriate with the old wine of ancient studies; these I nourish
with the fruit of grammatical knowledge; in the eyes of these
again I seek to make bright the courses of the stars. . . . But I
have need of the most excellent books of scholastic learning,
which I had procured in my own country, either by the devoted
care of my master, or by my own labours. I therefore beseech
your majesty . . . to permit me to send certain of our household
to bring over into France the flowers of Britain, that the garden
of Paradise may not be confined to York, but may send some of
its scions to Tours." What the "flowers of Britan" were at this
time Alcuin has told us in Latin verse. At York, "where he sowed
the seeds of knowledge in the morning of his life," thou shalt
find, he rimes:—

"The volumes that contain
All the ancient fathers who remain;
There all the Latin writers make their home
With those that glorious Greece transferred to Rome,—
The Hebrews draw from their celestial stream,
And Africa is bright with learning's beam."

Then, after including in his metrical catalogue the names of forty writers, he proceeds:—

"There shalt thou find, O reader, many more
Famed for their style, the masters of old lore,
Whose many volumes singly to rehearse
Were far too tedious for our present verse."

A goodly store indeed in such an age.

Carolingian Renaissance

The encouragement which Charles the Great gave in the late eighth century to scholars from England, Ireland, and Italy culminated in the so-called Carolingian Renaissance. Charlemagne, before his coronation as Emperor of the Holy Roman Empire in 800, had sent first to Fulda and then to other monasteries a letter on the Pursuit of Learning which stressed the need for literacy and understanding among their monks. The Carolingian Age emphasized a fresh study of the writings of the Church Fathers and of the Latin poets and prose writers of pagan Rome. This rediscovery of the classics in Latin stimulated intense activity in collecting manuscripts on the part of the writing schools in Continental cathedrals and monasteries.

Charles the Great enjoyed being read to (whether he could read is disputed), but he found more delight in the conversation of the scholars attached to his court at Aachen or with him on campaigns. Outstanding among this group was Alcuin who had come from York to head Charles's palace school, the purpose of which was to prepare the sons of Frankish nobles for careers at court or in the Church. The assembled scholars taught in the school, yet found time to read Latin authors, to collect manuscripts, and to compose poems, grammars, and histories. Besides Alcuin, Charlemagne's court included Einhard, biographer of the Emperor, who studied the Church Fathers and pagan writers until he could write commendable classical Latin; Ebbo, who left Aachen in 816 to establish a school at Rheims which produced many notable manuscripts; and Reginbert, librarian of the great collection of literature at Reichenau.

After the death of Charlemagne in 814, his brilliant court rapidly declined. Intellectual activities once again became centered in the monasteries, and the old patterns were soon revived: Latin was taught, manuscripts were copied, and religious treatises were composed. During the ninth century, learned monks in one monastery frequently made contact with scholars in another. Those in the Frankish kingdom attracted many of the English and Irish monks who had fled before the Viking invaders in their home countries. The refugees often brought with them books as well as special talents and experiences which enriched the intellectual life of monasteries on the Continent.

Late in the ninth century, learning continued to hold a high place in the abbey at Ferrières in France. The abbot, Lupus, surnamed Servatus, wrote a revealing letter to Einhard after reading his Life of Charles the Great. Part of his letter, as quoted in Eleanor Shipley Duckett's Carolingian Portraits: A Study in the Ninth Century (Ann Arbor: University of Michigan Press, 1962), pp. 165–166, reads:

> I have loved books since I was a little boy. Never have I despised them, in the fashion of so many people of our times, as a frivolous indulgence of leisure hours. . . .
>
> In the days of Charles the Emperor, as you must be well aware, the desire for knowledge did revive for a while. Nowadays those who want to learn are a burden upon society.

Lupus enlarged the Ferrières abbey library through borrowing manuscripts from individuals such as Einhard and from monasteries at Fulda, Tours, and elsewhere, and in 855 he requested Pope Benedict III to lend him Cicero's Orations, Quintilian's Institutions, and Donatus's Commentary on Terence so that he could make copies. He even borrowed second copies of books so that he could collate and correct those in his abbey. Lupus once sought to obtain a copy of a book by St. Jerome from the abbot at York, because he believed that the work was longer than the text at hand. Not satisfied with the response from York, Lupus proceeded to ask Benedict III to send the book from his great library in Rome.

The spirit of the Carolingian Age lingered until late in the tenth century in the person of Gerbert, who was to become Sylvester II when elevated to the papacy by a former student, Otto III. When Otto became king of the Germans in 983 he also became emperor of the Holy Roman Empire, an office which Charlemagne had been the first to hold, almost two centuries earlier. The future pope's scholarly efforts are presented in a long article by Roland Allen on "Gerbert, Pope Silvester II," The English Historical Review, October 1892, pp. 626–631 and 634–635.

Gerbert was born of humble parentage in the province of Aquitaine, probably about the year 945. The story of his early life lies hidden in the deepest obscurity. He was brought up in the monastery of St. Gerauld at Aurillac, where he studied grammar under the monk Raymond. Of his life there we know only the closing scene. About the year 967, Borel, count of Barcelona and duke of the Spanish march, came to Aurillac on a pilgrimage. Asked whether there were in his country men skilled in the arts, he readily answered that there were. Thereupon he was persuaded by the abbot to take one of the young monks, to be instructed in the arts, and Gerbert was chosen to go with him. Borel placed him under the charge of Hatto, bishop of Vich, with whom he obtained a thorough knowledge of mathematics. . . .

The church in the Spanish march had at this time no metropolitan of its own, but looked for governance to the primate of Narbonne. Borel, in order to free his country from such dependence, was anxious to found an archbishopric at Vich, and, to procure this boon from the pope, set out for Rome in the year 970, taking with him Hatto and Gerbert. There Pope John XIII, struck with Gerbert's mathematical knowledge, pointed him out to the emperor Otto I. Otto was interested: he asked Gerbert what he knew, and, hearing in reply that he knew sufficient mathematics but wished to learn logic, took him into his court until a suitable teacher could be found. Meanwhile he employed him in teaching the young men of his suite. Gerbert's anxiety to learn logic was soon to be satisfied. He had been scarcely a year in Italy when there arrived from France, as ambassador from King Lothar, Garamnus, archdeacon of Rheims, who was held to be a great logician. Gerbert obtained leave to attend this man, and followed him to Rheims, where he arrived about the year 972.

Here he was welcomed with the greatest joy by Adalbero, the archbishop, who, formerly canon of Metz, had been appointed to the archbishopric of Rheims in 962. Adalbero had found the church in a very demoralised state. Under the rule of his predecessor all discipline had been relaxed; the monks dressed and behaved in a most licentious way. The account of a synod held soon after his consecration gives a most interesting picture of the freedom which was sometimes allowed to the religious. Under Adalbero's energetic rule all was changed. He restored the cathedral; he ordered the canons, who were living each in his own house, to live together in common, and caused them to keep the canonical hours; he ordered the monks to live chastely, to abandon their strange garments, and to live according to rule. Finally he journeyed to Rome, to procure privileges for his monasteries. Not content with this, he proceeded to reform his schools, for he thought it well that the sons of the church should receive instruction in useful studies. It was at this moment that he met Gerbert, with whom he formed a firm friendship which lasted until his death in 989.

As schoolmaster of Rheims Gerbert now entered upon what was probably the happiest, as it was certainly the most peaceful, period of his life—ten years spent in the collection of a splendid library, in the laborious copying of books, in the introduction of new methods of study, and in the invention of many ingenious instruments. From the first the whole tenor of his teaching was strictly opposed to the tendency of the reformation, which, begun by St. Odo at Cluny, had spread to most of the great monastic schools. St. Odo had been warned in a dream not to continue the reading of Virgil, and of the other poets, of which he had been inordinately fond. Henceforward the classics were viewed with disfavour by the abbots who adopted his reform. They were not entirely rejected, for Abbo of Fleury had read Virgil, Horace, Juvenal, and Persius; but they were shunned as dangerous, and sometimes poems were mutilated until they lost all their unity and beauty. The whole teaching of the monastic schools was but a training for the study of holy scripture and of the fathers, and the masters feared lest love for the classics should draw away their pupils from that supreme object. So strong was this feeling that, at the beginning of the eleventh century, young men, on entering the cloister, were said to leave liberal studies behind them. M. Pfister, noting the frequency with which we are told that abbots refused to allow their monks to read the classics, and considering how often copies of the poets were destroyed that the parchment might be used again, declares that the ancient writers had no worse enemies, in the tenth century, than the monks, than those especially who had undergone the reform of Cluny.

Gerbert's whole course of lectures was a protest against this rejection of the classics. His object was to train his pupils for an active, not for a contemplative life. He gives as the purpose of skilful speaking, not the delight of the hearers, but the power of guiding and restraining the rash impulses of an excited mob. For this training in speaking he knew no better way than the study of the best models, and therefore he laid great stress upon the reading and explanation of the best Latin classics, a practice which gave such zest and reality to his teaching that, added to his intuitive power of attaching his pupils to him, it soon made him the most popular teacher in Gaul. Gerbert was thus doing in Gaul the work which St. Bruno had done for Otto I in Germany. St. Bruno aimed at providing men fit to occupy those offices of state which were then attached to the great archbishoprics. To fulfil the duties which these offices entailed it was necessary that the archbishop should be something more than a mere ecclesiastic; he must have read more widely than could be done in the monastic schools. St. Bruno, therefore, restored the great ecclesiastical schools, and made his object the training of men for affairs of state. In the same way, though not perhaps with so definite an object, Gerbert, by widening the usual course of study and making it as practical as possible, did much to raise up men capable of holding offices which called for great administrative ability. This fact it is which accounts for the large number of his pupils who became famous as administrators and as founders of schools.

His course of lectures and manner of teaching are set forth by his pupil Richer in his history. He adopted the plan which was universally accepted, and lectured on all the seven arts. Beginning with the rudimentary arts of the trivium, he instructed his pupils in grammar, which is defined as the art of explaining the poets and historians, and of speaking and writing correctly. Then advancing to dialectic, he read and explained clearly Porphyry's "Isagoge," using the translation of Victorinus as his text-book, supplemented by the commentary of Boethius; after this Aristotle's "Categories" and Cicero's "Topics," still using the commentaries of Boethius. Before proceeding to rhetoric he caused his pupils to read carefully the best Latin poets, because he saw that, without understanding the methods of speech which are to be learned in the poets, it was impossible to arrive at skill in oratory. In this way they became thoroughly conversant with Virgil, Statius, Terence, Juvenal, Persius, Horace, and Lucan. After this they practiced before him controversial exercises.

With their minds well trained in these exercises his pupils advanced to the higher arts of the quadrivium—arithmetic, music, astronomy, and geometry. Here it was that Gerbert's powers found their fullest play in inventions of all kinds for the simplification of the subject and the advancement of science. . . .

Gerbert's insatiable thirst after knowledge led him to search everywhere for books, which were at this time very rare and costly. Many causes may be assigned for this scarceness: the turbulence of the age drew away men's minds from the quiet toil of the study; the constant inroads of the pirates swept away monasteries and libraries together; the costliness of parchment and the difficulty of communication all combined to render books of the utmost value. But Gerbert's diligence overcame every difficulty. He had regular correspondents in many of the great cities of Europe, to whom he applied for any book which might fall into their hands; he spared neither money nor pains to procure copies of the great classical authors; his letters teem with allusions to and requests for books. For Remigius, a monk of Trier, he made one of his spheres, a matter of no small labour to one so occupied in civil business, in order to procure in return a copy of the "Achilleid" of Statius. It is curious to note that, after leaving Bobbio, he asks for copies of only three books; yet Bobbio contained one of the best libraries of the tenth century. So well had he stocked his library at Rheims.

Such was the extent of Gerbert's knowledge, such was his library. We can scarcely wonder, then, that his fame spread not only through Gaul, but to all the nations of Germany, and that pupils thronged to him from every side.

Although the spirit of the so-called Carolingian Renaissance is apparent in the career of Gerbert, who lived until the beginning of the eleventh century, Charlemagne's empire, which had been formed in the late eighth and early ninth centuries, had disintegrated under the weak rule of his sons and grandsons and the divisive pressures of feudalism. Charlemagne, who had brought much of Western Europe into a new Holy Roman Empire, became a hero of legends and romances, and the level of culture which prevailed at his court has enjoyed a reputation which probably exceeds its accomplishments and influence. After the ninth century, libraries in the old Benedictine monasteries stagnated, and most notable library developments of the eleventh and twelfth centuries occurred at cathedral schools and episcopal seats.

Most monastic libraries comprised small collections including a Bible, the writings of leading Church Fathers (Augustine and Jerome were favorites), and copies of books by popular ancient writers, especially Vergil and Ovid. The manuscripts, which seldom numbered more than a few hundred, ordinarily were kept in chests, but improved book production in the late Middle Ages led to larger collections which were shelved in presses, on rows of desks, and in a few institutions in a separate room or hall provided for the purpose. The use made of monastery collections is summarized in these paragraphs from the article by Herbert Thurston on "Libraries," The Catholic Encyclopedia IX (1910): 230–231:

> Speaking of Western Europe as a whole, we may regard it as an undisputed principle throughout the Middle Ages that a library of some sort was an essential part of every monastic establishment. "Claustrum sine armario, castrum sine armamentario," ran the adage; that is to say, a monastery without a library is a fort without an armoury. In all the developments of the Benedictine

Rule, regulations of some kind are laid down for the use of books. We may quote, for example, the directions given by Lanfranc for the annual calling-in of library books on the first Sunday of Lent. The monks are bidden to bring back all books to the chapter house, and thereupon, "let the librarian read a document [*breve*] setting forth the names of the brethren who have had books during the past year; and let each brother when he hears his own name pronounced, return the book which has been entrusted to him for reading, and let him who is conscious of not having read the book through which he has received, fall down on his face, confess his fault, and pray for forgiveness. And let the aforesaid librarian hand to each brother another book for reading; and when the books have been distributed in order, let the aforesaid librarian in the same chapter put on record the names of the books and of those who receive them."

J. W. Clark gives a summary of the arrangements peculiar to the different orders. Both the Cluniacs and Benedictines, he says, put the books in charge of the precentor, often also styled *armarius*, and there is to be an annual audit and registration similar to that just described. Among the later Benedictines we also find a further regulation that the precentor is to keep all in repair and personally to supervise the daily use of the manuscripts, restoring each to its proper place when done with. Among these later Benedictine rules, as found, for example, at Abingdon at the end of the twelfth century, first appears the important permission to lend books to others outside the monastery on receipt of an adequate pledge. The Carthusians also maintained the principle of lending. As for the monks themselves, each brother might have two books, and he is to be specially careful to keep them clean. Among the Cistercians a particular official has charge of the books, about the safety of which great care is to be taken, and at certain times of the day he is to lock the press. This last regulation is also observed by the Premonstratensians, who further require their librarian to take note of books borrowed as well as books lent. Finally, the Augustinians, who are very full in their directions regarding the use of the library, also permit books to be lent outside, but insist much on the need of proper security (see Clark, "Care of Books," 58–73).

The importance of the permission to lend consists, of course, in this: that the monasteries thus became the public libraries of the surrounding district and diffused much more widely the benefit afforded by their own command of books. The practice no doubt involved much risk of loss, and there was a disposition sometimes manifested to forbid the lending of books altogether. On the other hand, it is clear that there were those who looked upon this means of helping their neighbours as a duty prescribed by the laws of charity. Thus, in 1212, a synod held in Paris passed the following decree: "We forbid those who belong to a religious order to formulate any vow against lending their books to those who are in need of them; seeing that to lend is enumerated among the principal works of mercy. After due consideration let some books be retained in the house for the use of the brethren; but let others according to the decision of the abbot be lent to those who are in need of them, the rights of the house being safeguarded. In future no penalty of anathema is to be attached to the removal of any book, and we annul and grant absolution from all anathemas of the sort" (Delisle in "Bib. de l'Ecole des Chartes," Ser. 3, I, 225). It is noteworthy, also, that in this same thirteenth century many volumes were bequeathed to the Augustinian house of St. Victor, Paris, on the express condition that they should be so lent. No doubt most of the lending was for the benefit of other monasteries, either for reading or, still more often, for the purpose of making a copy. Against the dangers thus incurred it would seem that some protection was sought by invoking anathemas upon the head of the faithless borrower. How far excommunications were seriously and validly enacted against the unlawful detainers of such volumes is a matter of some uncertainty, but, as in the case of Ashur-ban-i-pal's cuneiform tablets, the manuscripts of medieval monasteries frequently contain on the fly-leaf some brief form of malediction against unjust possessors or detainers. For example, in a Jumièges book we find: "Should anyone by craft or any device whatever abstract this book from this place [Jumièges] may his soul suffer in retribution for what he has done, and may his name be erased from the book of the living and not be recorded among the Blessed." But in general such formulae were more compendious, as, for example, the following found in many St. Alban's books: "This book belongs to St. Alban. May whoever steals it from him or erases his inscription of ownership [titulum deleverit] be anathema. Amen."

The monastic libraries which flourished from the sixth until the tenth century helped to transmit classical civilization to the modern world, yet one of the most thorough students of monasticism, Dom M. D. Knowles, observed in "The Preservation of the Classics," in The English Library before 1700 by Francis Wormald and C. E. Wright (London: University of London, 1958), p. 147:

> No attempt was ever made or even imagined to make a complete collection of the classics. On a balance, immeasurable as is the benefit they conferred on posterity in this respect, the monasteries have probably received somewhat more than their share of praise from recent historians.

Later Middle Ages

"The Benedictine age of Western culture," in which monks preserved and copied Christian and pagan books for their own edification, was engulfed in the late Middle Ages by circumstances such as the rise of the friars, the establishment of universities, and the growth of medieval towns. The friars, for example, in their work with the new universities, required books in natural sciences and in systematic theology. This led to the production and acquisition of volumes different from those found in early monastic libraries. Students in medieval universities did buy books, but they could not afford many and were obliged to borrow volumes from their college libraries. At the Sorbonne, which was formally organized in 1289, fellows could not enter the library except in proper academic attire because it was considered to be "a holy and august place."

During the High Middle Ages, the largest and most distinguished libraries were usually located in cathedrals or in the residences of high churchmen, and many of their holdings are known from catalogues which have survived. Outstanding among the libraries of the later Middle Ages are those in the cathedral at Verona, in the abbey at Monte Cassino in Italy, in the German cathedral at Bamberg (estab-

Plate V Scribe at Work

lished in 1007 by Henry II), in the cathedrals at Rheims and Chartres in France, and at the monastery at Bec in Normandy, under the leadership of Lanfranc, whose pupils rose to positions of prominence in France, Italy, and England.

Lanfranc, who was born at Pavia about the year 1000, became the first Archbishop of Canterbury after the Norman conquest of England. Shortly after his arrival at Canterbury, Lanfranc introduced new rules for the monks, which allotted more hours for study, and he issued minute regulations for the lending and reading of books at Christ Church. In addition to Lanfranc's library, there was a second notable collection in Canterbury at St. Augustine's Abbey. The cathedrals at Rochester, at Lincoln (under the dynamic and scholarly Bishop Robert Grosseteste), at Hereford, and at Durham had remarkable libraries in the late Middle Ages. Also important were the libraries in the abbeys at St. Albans, Westminster, York, and elsewhere. Numerous details about these collections which flourished during the High Middle Ages in Italy, Germany, France, and England are brought together in lengthy chapters on the libraries in each of the four principal countries in Western Europe in James Westfall Thompson's The Medieval Library (Chicago: University of Chicago Press, 1939), pp. 136–309.

The best known work on book collecting produced during the Middle Ages, the Philobiblon, appeared early in the fourteenth century in England. This essay, usually attributed to Richard Aungerville deBury, Bishop of Durham from 1333–1345, has continued in succeeding centuries to attract readers because of its author's intimate and candid presentation. DeBury relates how he utilized his connections as a churchman and courtier to enlarge his store of books, and he devotes separate chapters to aspects of his subject such as the importance of books and the superiority of ancient authors. The Philobiblon is a product of the late Middle Ages, but the voice of Richard deBury is that of a humanist in the Renaissance which was then dawning in Italy. Here is E. C. Thomas's translation of Richard deBury's brief chapter on the custody of books, from The Love of Books: The Philobiblon (London: Alexander Moring, 1903), pp. 104–109:

> We are not only rendering service to God in preparing volumes of new books, but also exercising an office of sacred piety when

Plate VI Seal of Richard deBury

we treat books carefully, and again when we restore them to their proper places and commend them to inviolable custody; that they may rejoice in purity while we have them in our hands, and rest securely when they are put back in their repositories. And surely next to the vestments and vessels dedicated to the Lord's body, holy books deserve to be rightly treated by the clergy, to which great injury is done so often as they are touched by unclean hands. Wherefore we deem it expedient to warn our students of various negligences, which might always be easily avoided and do wonderful harm to books.

And in the first place as to the opening and closing of books, let there be due moderation, that they be not unclasped in precipitate haste, nor when we have finished our inspection be put away without being duly closed. For it behooves us to guard a book much more carefully than a boot.

But the race of scholars is commonly badly brought up, and unless they are bridled in by the rules of their elders they indulge in infinite puerilities. They behave with petulance, and are puffed up with presumption, judging of everything as if they were certain, though they are altogether inexperienced.

You may happen to see some headstrong youth lazily lounging over his studies, and when the winter's frost is sharp, his nose running from the nipping cold drips down, nor does he think of wiping it with his pocket-handkerchief until he has bedewed the book before him with the ugly moisture. Would that he had before him no book, but a cobbler's apron! His nails are stuffed with fetid filth as black as jet, with which he marks any passage that pleases him. He distributes a multitude of straws, which he inserts to stick out in different places, so that the halm may remind him of what his memory cannot retain. These straws, because the book has no stomach to digest them, and no one takes them out, first distend the book from its wonted closing, and at length, being carelessly abandoned to oblivion, go to decay. He does not fear to eat fruit or cheese over an open book, or carelessly to carry a cup to and from his mouth; and because he has no wallet at hand he drops into books the fragments that are left. Continually chattering, he is never weary of disputing with his companions, and while he alleges a crowd of senseless arguments, he wets the book lying half open in his lap with sputtering showers. Aye, and then hastily folding his arms he leans forward on the book, and by a brief spell of study invites a prolonged nap; and then, by way of mending the wrinkles, he folds back the margin of the leaves, to the no small injury of the book. Now the rain is over and gone, and the flowers have appeared in our land. Then the scholar we are speaking of, a neglecter rather than an inspecter of books, will stuff his volume with violets, and primroses, with roses and quatrefoil. Then he will use his wet and perspiring hands to turn over the volumes; then he will thump the white vellum with gloves covered with all kinds of dust, and with his finger clad in long-used leather will hunt line by line through the page; then at the sting of the biting flea the sacred book is flung aside, and is hardly shut for another month, until it is so full of the dust that has found its way within, that it resists the effort to close it.

But the handling of books is specially to be forbidden to those shameless youths, who as soon as they have learned to form the shapes of letters, straightway, if they have the opportunity, become unhappy commentators, and wherever they find an extra margin about the text, furnish it with monstrous alphabets, or if any other frivolity strikes their fancy, at once their pen begins to write it. There the Latinist and sophister and every unlearned writer tries the fitness of his pen, a practice that we have frequently seen injuring the usefulness and value of the most beautiful books.

Again, there is a class of thieves shamefully mutilating books, who cut away the margins from the sides to use as material for letters, leaving only the text, or employ the leaves from the ends, inserted for the protection of the book, for various uses and abuses—a kind of sacrilege which should be prohibited by the threat of anathema.

Again, it is part of the decency of scholars that whenever they return from meals to their study, washing should invariably precede reading, and that no grease-stained finger should unfasten the clasps, or turn the leaves of a book. Nor let a crying child admire the pictures in the capital letters, lest he soil the parchment with wet fingers; for a child instantly touches whatever he sees. Moreover, the laity, who look at a book turned upside down just as if it were open in the right way, are utterly unworthy of any communion with books. Let the clerk take care also that the smutty scullion reeking from his stewpots does not touch the lily leaves of books, all unwashed, but he who walketh without blemish shall minister to the precious volumes. And, again, the cleanliness of decent hands would be of great benefit to books as well as scholars, if it were not that the itch and pimples are characteristic of the clergy.

Whenever defects are noticed in books, they should be promptly repaired, since nothing spreads more quickly than a tear and a rent which if neglected at the time will have to be repaired afterwards with usury.

Moses, the gentlest of men, teaches us to make bookcases most neatly, wherein they may be protected from any injury: *Take, he says, this book of the law, and put it in the side of the ark of the covenant of the Lord your God.* O fitting place and appropriate for a library, which was made of imperishable shittim-wood, and was all covered within and without with gold! But the Saviour also has warned us by His example against all unbecoming carelessness in the handling of books, as we read in S. Luke. For when He had read the scriptural prophecy of Himself in the book that was delivered to Him, He did not give it again to the minister, until He had closed it with his own most sacred hands. By which students are most clearly taught that in the care of books the merest trifles ought not to be neglected.

The Renaissance

During the fourteenth and fifteenth centuries, the towns became the intellectual centers of Europe, and monastic libraries suffered from neglect. Even in some of the most famous houses, such as St. Gall and Fulda, few monks knew how to write; consequently, very little copying of manuscripts was done, and many of the books once treasured in monastic libraries were scattered. The centuries marked by the stagnation of the monasteries were succeeded by the bright and vigorous period in European history known as the Renaissance, which found its initial impulse in Italy in the study of ancient manuscripts and art.

The Age of the Renaissance brought profound economic and political changes, and men came to be recognized as individuals with limitless capacities; witness Hamlet's exclamation, "What a piece of work is a man! how noble in reason! how infinite in faculty!" Two notable developments of the fifteenth century, the invention of printing from movable type and the discovery of the Western Hemisphere, had tremendous impact on the lives of Europeans, but the roles played in the history of libraries by the introduction of the printed book and the Age of Exploration will not be considered in this section. Instead, the manuscript book, which for four millennia had provided Western civilization with a means of communication transcending distance and time, will continue to hold the center of the stage throughout this treatment of the Renaissance.

Italy

The Renaissance was viewed for a time as the bright dawn after the Dark Ages, but this interpretation ignores the intellectual accomplishments of ten centuries. The books of ancient authors, which aroused a zest for learning in the Italian humanists, came principally from monasteries where they had been cherished and copied from the time of Cassiodorus and St. Benedict. In Germany alone there were several thousand monastic libraries which contained such a wealth of books by ancient writers that one of the foremost Italian book hunters characterized the country as "a prison where Roman classics were held captive by Teutonic barbarians."

The New Learning found its first champion in Petrarch, Italian poet of the fourteenth century, who inspired Boccaccio, Salutate, and other early Italian humanists to seek and study classical writings. Petrarch's life as a humanist and book collector is sketched in Charles and Mary Elton's The Great Book-Collectors (London: Kegan Paul, 1893), pp. 41–44 and 48–52:

> The enlightenment of an age of ignorance cannot be attributed to any single person; yet it has been said with some justice, that as the mediaeval darkness lifted, one figure was seen standing in advance, and that Petrarch was rightly hailed as "the harbinger of day." His fame rests not so much on his poems as upon his incessant labours in the task of educating his countrymen. Petrarch was devoted to books from his boyhood. His youth was passed near Avignon, "on the banks of the windy Rhone." After receiving the ordinary instruction in grammar and rhetoric, he passed four years at Montpellier, and proceeded to study law at Bologna. "I kept my terms in Civil Law," he said, "and made some progress; but I gave up the subject on becoming my own master, not because I disliked the Law, which no doubt is full of the Roman learning, but because it is so often perverted by evil-minded men." He seems to have worked for a time under his friend Cino of Pistoia, and to have attended the lectures of the jurist Andrea,

whose daughter Novella is said to have sometimes taken the class "with a little curtain in front of her beautiful face." While studying at Bologna, Petrarch made his first collection of books instead of devoting himself to the Law. His old father once paid him a visit and began burning the parchments on a funeral pile: the boy's supplications and promises saved the poor remainder. He tried hard to follow his father's practical advice, but always in vain; "Nature called him in another direction, and it is idle to struggle against her."

On Petrarch's return to Avignon he obtained the friendship of Cardinal Colonna: and here the whole course of his life was fixed when he first saw Laura "in a green dress embroidered with violets." Her face was stamped upon his mind, and haunted him through all efforts at repose: and perhaps it is to her influence that he owed his rank among the lyrical poets and the crown bestowed at Rome. His whole life was thenceforth devoted to the service of the book. He declared that he had the writing-disease, and was the victim of a general epidemic. "All the world is taking up the writer's part, which ought to be confined to a few: the number of the sick increases and the disease becomes daily more virulent." A victim of the mania himself, he laughs at his own misfortune: yet it might have been better, he thought, to have been a labourer or a weaver at the loom. "There are several kinds of melancholia: and some madmen will write books, just as others toss pebbles in their hands." As for literary fame, it is but a harvest of thin air, "and it is only fit for sailors to watch a breeze and to whistle for a wind."

Petrarch collected books in many parts of Europe. In 1329, when he was twenty-five years of age, he made a tour through Switzerland to the cities of Flanders. The Flemish schools had lost something of their ancient fame since the development of the University of Paris. Several fine collections of books were still preserved in the monasteries. The Abbey of Laubes was especially rich in biblical commentaries and other works of criticism, which were all destroyed afterwards in a fire, except a Vulgate of the eighth century that happened to be required for use at the Council of Trent. Petrarch described his visit to Liège in a letter to a friend; "When we arrived I heard that there was a good supply of books, so I kept all my party there until I had one oration of Cicero transcribed by a colleague, and another in my own writing, which I afterwards published in Italy; but in that fair city of the barbarians it was very difficult to get any ink, and what I did procure was as yellow as saffron."

A few years afterwards he went from Avignon to Paris, and was astonished at the net-work of filthy lanes in the students' quarter. It was a paradise of books, all kept at fair prices by the University's decree; but the traveller declared that, except in "the world's sink" at Avignon, he had never seen so dirty a place. At Rome he was dismayed to find that all the books were the prey of the foreigner. The English and French merchants were carrying away what had been spared by the Goths and Vandals. "Are you not ashamed," he cried to his Roman friends, "are you not ashamed that your avarice should allow these strangers every day to acquire some remnant of your ancient majesty?" . . .

Petrarch was in truth a careless custodian of his prisoners. He was too ready to lend a book to a friend, and his generosity on one occasion caused a serious loss to literature. The only known copy of a treatise by Cicero was awaiting transcription in his library; but he allowed it to be carried off by an old scholar in need of assistance: it was pledged in some unknown quarter, and nothing was ever heard again of the precious deposit.

He returned to Avignon in 1337, and made himself a quiet home at Vaucluse. His letters are full of allusions to his little farm, to the poplars in the horse-shoe valley, and the river brimming out from the "monarch of springs." In these new lawns of Helicon he made a new home for his books, and tried to forget in their company the tumults that had driven him from Italy. In 1340 he received offers of a laureate's crown from Rome, the capital of the world, and from Paris, "the birth-place of learning." "I start to-day," he wrote to Colonna, "to receive my reward over the graves of those who were the pride of ancient Rome, and in the very theatre of their exploits." The Capitol resounded to such cheers that its walls and "antique dome" seemed to share in the public joy: the senator placed a chaplet on his brow, and old Stephen Colonna added a few words of praise amid the applause of the Roman people.

At Parma, soon afterwards, Petrarch formed another library which he called his "second Parnassus." At Padua he busied himself in the education of an adopted son, the young John of Ravenna, who lived to be a celebrated professor, and was nick-named "the Trojan Horse," because he turned out so many ex-cellent Grecians. In a cottage near Milan the poet received a visit from Boccaccio, who was at that time inclined to renounce the world. He offered to give his whole library to Petrarch: he did afterwards send to his host a *Dante* of his own copying, which is now preserved in the Vatican. The approach of a pesti-lence led Petrarch to remove his home to Venice: and here he was again visited by Boccaccio, this time in company with Leontio Pilato, a Calabrian Greek trading in books between Italy and Constantinople.

Leontio was the translator of Homer, and expounded his poems from the Chair of Rhetoric at Florence. He was a man of forbidding appearance, and "more obdurate," said Petrarch, "than the rocks that he will encounter in his voyage": "fearing that I might catch his bad temper, I let him go, and gave him a Terence to amuse him on the way, though I do not know what this melancholy Greek could have in common with that lively African." Leontio was killed by lightning on his return voyage; and there was much anxiety until it could be ascertained that his literary stock-in-trade had been rescued from the hands of the sailors. It was not till the end of the century that Chrysoloras renewed the knowledge of the classics: but we may regard the austere Leontio as the chief precursor of the crowd of later immi-grants, each with a gem, or bronze, or "a brown Greek manu-script" for sale, and all eager to play their parts in the restoration of learning.

Towards the end of his life Petrarch became tired of carrying his books about. When he broke up the libraries at Parma and Vaucluse he had formed the habit of travelling with bales of manuscripts in a long cavalcade; but he determined afterwards to offer the collection to Venice, on condition that it should be properly housed, and should never be sold or divided. The offer was accepted by the Republic, and the Palazzo Molina was assigned as a home for the poet and his books. Petrarch, however, had other plans for himself. He wished to be near Padua, where he held a canonry; and he accordingly built himself a cottage at Arquà, among the Euganean Hills, about ten miles from the city. A few olive-trees and a little vine-yard sufficed for the wants of his modest household; and there, as he wrote to his brother, broken in body but easy in his mind, he passed his time in reading, and prepared for his end. His only regret was that there was no monastery near in which he might see his beloved Gerard fulfilling his religious duties. He seems to have given up his love for fine books with other worldly vanities. He offers excuses for the plain appearance of a volume of "St. Augustine" which he was sending as a present. "One must not," said he, "expect perfect manuscripts from scholars who are engaged on better things. A general does not sharpen the soldiers' swords. Apelles did not cut out his own boards, or Polycletus his sheets of ivory; some humble person always prepares the material on which a higher mind is to be engaged. So is it with books: some polish the parchment, and others copy or correct the text; others again do the illumination, to use the common phrase; but a loftier spirit will disdain these menial occupations." The scholar's books are often of a rough and neglected appearance, for abundance of anything makes the owner "careless and secure"; it is the invalid who is particular about every breath of air, but the strong man loves the rough breeze. "As to this book of the *Confessions*, its first aspect will teach you all about it. Quite new, quite unadorned, untouched by the corrector's fangs, it comes out of my young servant's hands. You will notice some defects in spelling, but no gross mistakes. In a word, you will perhaps find things in it which will exercise but not disturb your understanding. Read it then, and ponder upon it. This book, which would enflame a heart of ice, must set your ardent soul on fire."

On a summer night of the year 1374, Petrarch died peacefully at Arquà, alone in his library. His few remaining books were sold, and some of them may still be seen in Rome and Paris. Those

Plate VII Petrarch's House at Arquà

which he had given to Venice suffered a strange reverse of fortune. How long the gift remained in the Palazzo Molina we cannot tell. We conjecture that it was discarded in the next century, before Bessarion presented his Greek books to the senate, and became the actual founder of the library of St. Mark. The antiquary Tomasini found Petrarch's books cast aside in a dark room behind the Horses of Lysippus. Some had crumbled into powder, and others had been glued into shapeless masses by the damp. The survivors were placed in the Libraria Vecchia, and are now in the Ducal Palace; but it was long before they were permitted to enter the building that sheltered the gift of Bessarion.

Petrarch's example of collecting manuscripts in the fourteenth century was followed by a host of other Italian scholars, book collectors, nobles, and churchmen. The work of Boccaccio, Pope Nicholas V, the dukes of Urbino, the Medici, and others is summarized in a chapter on "The Old Authors" in Jacob Burckhardt's The Civilisation of the Renaissance in Italy *(London: Sonnenschein, 1904), pp. 187–194:*

> Great as was the influence of the old writers on the Italian mind in the fourteenth century and before, yet that influence was due rather to the wide diffusion of what had long been known, than to the discovery of much that was new. The most popular Latin poets, historians, orators, and letter-writers, together with a number of Latin translations of single works of Aristotle, Plutarch, and a few other Greek authors, constituted the treasure from which a few favoured individuals in the time of Petrarch and Boccaccio drew their inspiration. The former, as is well known, owned and kept with religious care a Greek Homer, which he was unable to read. A complete Latin translation of the "Iliad" and "Odyssey," though a very bad one, was made at Petrarch's suggestion and with Boccaccio's help by a Calabrian Greek, Leonzio Pilato. But with the fifteenth century began the long list of new discoveries, the systematic creation of libraries by means of copies, and the rapid multiplication of translations from the Greek.
>
> Had it not been for the enthusiasm of a few collectors of that

age, who shrank from no effort or privation in their researches, we should certainly possess only a small part of the literature, especially that of the Greeks, which is now in our hands. Pope Nicholas V, when only a simple monk, ran deeply into debt through buying manuscripts or having them copied. Even then he made no secret of his passion for the two great interests of the Renaissance, books and buildings. As Pope he kept his word. Copyists wrote and spies searched for him through half the world. Perotto received 500 ducats for the Latin translation of Polybius; Guarino, 1,000 gold florins for that of Strabo, and he would have been paid 500 more but for the death of the Pope. Filelfo was to have received 10,000 gold florins for a metrical translation of Homer, and was only prevented by the Pope's death from coming from Milan to Rome. Nicholas left a collection of 5,000, or, according to another way of calculating, of 9,000 volumes, for the use of the members of the Curia, which became the foundation of the library of the Vatican. It was to be preserved in the palace itself, as its noblest ornament, like the library of Ptolemy Philadelphus at Alexandria. When the plague (1450) drove him and his court to Fabriano, whence then, as now, the best paper was procured, he took his translators and compilers with him, that he might run no risk of losing them.

The Florentine Niccolò Niccoli, a member of that accomplished circle of friends which surrounded the elder Cosimo de Medici, spent his whole fortune in buying books. At last, when his money was all gone, the Medici put their purse at his disposal for any sum which his purpose might require. We owe to him the completion of Ammianus Marcellinus, of the "De Oratore" of Cicero, the text of Lucretius which still has most authority, and other works; he persuaded Cosimo to buy the best manuscript of Pliny from a monastery at Lübeck. With noble confidence he lent his books to those who asked for them, allowed all comers to study them in his own house, and was ready to converse with the students on what they had read. His collection of 800 volumes, valued at 6,000 gold florins, passed after his death, through Cosimo's intervention, to the monastery of San Marco, on the condition that it should be accessible to the public, and is now one of the jewels of the Laurentian library.

Of the two great book-finders, Guarino and Poggio, the latter, on the occasion of the Council of Constanz and acting partly as the agent of Niccoli, searched industriously among the abbeys of South Germany. He there discovered six orations of Cicero, and the first complete Quintilian, that of St. Gall, now at Zürich; in thirty-two days he is said to have copied the whole of it in a beautiful handwriting. He was able to make important additions to Silius Italicus, Manilius, Lucretius, Valerius Flaccus, Asconius Pedianus, Columella, Celsus, Aulus Gellius, Statius, and others; and with the help of Lionardo Aretino he unearthed the last twelve comedies of Plautus, as well as the Verrine orations, the "Brutus" and the "De Oratore" of Cicero.

The famous Greek, Cardinal Bessarion, in whom patriotism was mingled with a zeal for letters, collected, at a great sacrifice (30,000 gold florins), 600 manuscripts of pagan and Christian authors. He then looked round for some receptacle where they could safely lie until his unhappy country, if she ever regained her freedom, could reclaim her lost literature. The Venetian government declared itself ready to erect a suitable building, and to this day the library of St. Mark retains a part of these treasures.

The formation of the celebrated Medicean library has a history of its own, into which we cannot here enter. The chief collector for Lorenzo Magnifico was Johannes Lascaris. It is well known that the collection, after the plundering in the year 1494, had to be recovered piecemeal by the Cardinal Giovanni Medici, afterwards Leo X.

The library of Urbino, now in the Vatican, was wholly the work of the great Frederick of Montefeltro. As a boy he had begun to collect; in after years he kept thirty or forty "scrittori" employed in various places, and spent in the course of time no less than 30,000 ducats on the collection. It was systematically extended and completed, chiefly by the help of Vespasiano, and his account of it forms an ideal picture of a library of the Renaissance. At Urbino there were catalogues of the libraries of the Vatican, of St. Mark at Florence, of the Visconti at Pavia, and even of the library at Oxford. It was noted with pride that in richness and completeness none could rival Urbino. Theology and the Middle Ages were perhaps most fully represented. There was a complete Thomas Aquinas, a complete Albertus Magnus, a complete Buonaventura. The collection, however, was a many-sided one, and included every work on medicine which was then to be had. Among the "moderns" the great writers of the fourteenth century—Dante and Boccaccio, with their complete works—occupied the first place. Then followed twenty-five select humanists, invariably with both their Latin and Italian writings and with all their translations. Among the Greek manuscripts the Fathers of the Church far outnumbered the rest; yet in the list of the classics we find all the works of Sophocles, all of Pindar, and all of Menander. The last must have quickly disappeared from Urbino, else the philologists would have soon edited it. There were men, however, in this book-collecting age who raised a warning voice against the vagaries of the passion. These were not the enemies of learning, but its friends, who feared that harm would come from a pursuit which had become a mania. Petrarch himself protested against the fashionable folly of a useless heaping up of books; and in the same century Giovanni Manzini ridiculed Andreolo de Ochis, a septuagenarian from Brescia, who was ready to sacrifice house and land, his wife and himself, to add to the stores of his library.

We have, further, a good deal of information as to the way in which manuscripts and libraries were multiplied. The purchase of an ancient manuscript, which contained a rare, or the only complete, or the only existing text of an old writer, was naturally a lucky accident of which we need take no further account. Among the professional copyists those who understood Greek took the highest place, and it was they especially who bore the honourable name of "scrittori." Their number was always limited, and the pay they received very large. The rest, simply called "copisti," were partly mere clerks who made their living by such work, partly schoolmasters and needy men of learning, who desired an addition to their income, partly monks, or even nuns, who regarded the pursuit as a work pleasing to God. In the early stages of the Renaissance the professional copyists were few and untrustworthy; their ignorant and dilatory ways were bitterly complained of by Petrarch. In the fifteenth century they were more numerous, and brought more knowledge to their calling, but in accuracy of work they never attained the conscientious precision of the old monks. They seem to have done their work in a sulky and perfunctory fashion, seldom putting their signatures at the foot of the codices, and showed no traces of that cheerful humour, or of that proud consciousness of a beneficent activity, which often surprises us in the French and German manuscripts of the same period. This is more curious, as the copyists at Rome in the time of Nicholas V were mostly Germans or Frenchmen—"barbarians" as the Italian humanists called them, probably men who were in search of favours at the papal court, and who kept themselves alive meanwhile by this means. When Cosimo de' Medici was in a hurry to form a library for his favourite foundation, the Badia below Fiesole, he sent for Vespasiano, and received from him the advice to give up all thoughts of purchasing books, since those which were worth getting could not be had easily, but rather to make use of the copyists; whereupon Cosimo bargained to pay him so much a day, and Vespasiano, with forty-five writers under him, delivered 200 volumes in twenty-two months. The catalogue of the works to be copied was sent to Cosimo by Nicholas V who wrote it with his own hand. Ecclesiastical literature and the books needed for the choral services naturally held the chief place in the list.

The handwriting was that beautiful modern Italian which was already in use in the preceding century, and which makes the sight of one of the books of that time a pleasure. Pope Nicholas V, Poggio, Giannozzo Manetti, Niccolò Niccoli, and other distinguished scholars, themselves wrote a beautiful hand, and desired and tolerated none other. The decorative adjuncts, even when miniatures formed no part of them, were full of taste, as may be seen especially in the Laurentian manuscripts, with the light and graceful scrolls which begin and end the lines. The material used to write on, when the work was ordered by great or wealthy people, was always parchment; the binding, both in the Vatican and at Urbino, was a uniform crimson velvet with silver clasps. Where there was so much care to show honour to the contents of a book by the beauty of its outward form, it is intelligible that the sudden appearance of printed books was greeted at first with anything but favour. The envoys of Cardinal Bessarion, when they saw for the first time a printed book in the house of Constantine Lascaris, laughed at the discovery "made among the barbarians in some German city," and Frederick of Urbino "would have been ashamed to own a printed book."

Foremost among the hunters of classical manuscripts was Poggio Bracciolini, whose discoveries are related in William Shepherd's The Life of Poggio Bracciolini *(London: T. Cadell, 1802), pp. 106–111:*

Poggio was far from being unconscious of the good service which he had done to the cause of letters, by the successful assiduity of his researches after the lost writers of antiquity. On the sixteenth of December of this year, he wrote to Guarino Veronese an epistle, in which, after duly extolling the importance and agreeable nature of the intelligence which he was about to announce, he gave him a particular account of the treasure which he had lately brought to light. From this letter it appears, that in consequence of information which Poggio had received, that a considerable number of books were deposited in the monastery of St. Gall, he took a journey to that town, accompanied by some of his friends. There they found a large number of manuscripts, and among the rest a complete copy of Quintilian, buried in rubbish and dust. For the books in question were not arranged in a library, but were thrown into the lowest apartment or dungeon of a tower, "Which," says Poggio, "was not even a fit residence for a condemned criminal." Besides Quintilian, they found in this obscure recess, the three first, and one half of the fourth books of the Argonautics of Valerius Flaccus, and Asconius Pedianus's comment on eight of Cicero's orations. The two latter manuscripts Poggio himself transcribed, with an intention of sending them to Leonardo Aretino, who, as appears by his letter quoted above, was so much elated by the revival of Quintilian, that he speaks of the discovery of Asconius and Flaccus as a matter of comparatively trifling moment.

Poggio zealously concurred in the wish of his friend Leonardo, to rescue from obscurity the lost works of Cicero. Nor were his endeavors to accomplish this valuable object entirely unsuccessful. In a monastery of the monks of Clugny, in the town of Langres, he found a copy of Cicero's Oration for Caecina, of which he made a transcript for the use of his Italian friends. In the course of various journies, which the vicissitudes of fortune obliged him to take at different periods of his life, he had the satisfaction to discover the following orations of the same author, the loss of which had been long deplored by the learned—De lege Agrariâ contra Rullum liber primus—Ejusdem liber secundus—Contra legem Agrariam ad populum—In L. Pisonem. A copy of these orations is preserved in the Abbey of Santa Maria, at Florence, to which is affixed a memorandum, which records the fact of their having been discovered by Poggio. This memorandum indeed makes mention of seven orations as having been found by him in France and Germany. . . .

Before the time of Poggio, eight only of the comedies of Plautus were known to the classical student. But by the industry or good fortune of one Nicolas of Treves, whom Poggio employed in continuing the researches in the monasteries of Germany, which he was unable to conduct in person, twelve more were brought to light. When Poggio had notice of this discovery, he was highly elated, and strenuously exhorted the cardinal Ursini to dispatch a trusty messenger to bring these valuable treasures to Rome. "I was not only solicitous, but importunate, with his eminence," says Poggio in a letter to Niccolò Niccoli, "to send somebody for the books." The cardinal did not however second the impatience of the Italian literati, who waited nearly two years before the manuscripts in question arrived in Rome, whither they were brought by Nicolas of Treves himself.

Besides Plautus's comedies, Nicolas of Treves brought to Rome a fragment of Aulus Gellius.

Poggio also found a copy of Julius Frontinus de Aquaeductis, and eight books of Firmicus's treatise on the mathematics, lying neglected and forgotten in the archives of the monastery of Monte Cassino; and at the instance of Niccolò Niccoli he prevailed upon the governors of that religious house, to allow him to convey these manuscripts to his own residence, for the purpose of decyphering and copying them. After he had transcribed Frontinus with his own hand, he returned the original manuscript to the library where it had been discovered. He also procured from Cologne the fifteenth book of Petronius Arbiter, a small fragment of which author he had before discovered in Britain. By his exertions also the entire work of Columella was brought to light, of which only fragments had been known to the earlier scholars. For the preservation of Calpurnius's Bucolic also, the republic of letters is indebted to the sagacious diligence of Poggio.

England

Although students of literature usually assume that the Renaissance reached England during the reign of Elizabeth I, Richard deBury, the author of Philobiblon, and Geoffrey Chaucer visited Italy during the time of Petrarch and Boccaccio. Early in the next century (the fifteenth), Humphrey, Duke of Gloucester, became familiar with the work of many Italian humanists, and he followed their example in collecting manuscripts of ancient authors. Humphrey's place in the history of libraries rests largely on the princely gifts he made to the young University of Oxford, which owned very few books when it appealed to the Duke for help early in the fifteenth century. The story is told in Kenneth H. Vickers's biography, Humphrey, Duke of Gloucester (London: Constable, 1907), pp. 402–407:

> Oxford had indeed fallen from her high estate, and was experiencing a period of affliction. The scholarship of the Middle Ages was worn out, the gospel of the New World had not yet been preached to her, but when, as in all its troubles, the University turned for help to the Duke of Gloucester, it had taken the first step towards better things. To him its grievances were told, and it was his generosity that resuscitated the lectures on the seven liberal arts and the three philosophies. Still, there was not sufficient for their continual maintenance. The lectures were carried on for some time, till the expense was more than could be borne, and again an appeal was made to the Duke. It was imperative

that they should have a permanent foundation for three more lecturers, and they must have books, and money to buy more. Yet another important corollary to these demands was that more suitable appointments should be made by those in authority in the kingdom, and that a man who had been educated at Oxford should not be at a disadvantage by reason of his superior knowledge. We have here the grievance in a nutshell. University education was unpopular, no one was ready to provide the means for that education, and the existing means were at present wholly inadequate.

Probably the lack of books was the greatest want, for beyond a very few volumes in the chests of the Library named after Bishop Cobham, and some others possessed by masters more wealthy than their fellows, there were no books at all in the University. The students had no access to books, all the teaching had to be done orally, and hence the knowledge acquired was of that purely hereditary type which could not be enlivened by the infusion of new ideas. To a lover and student of books such as Duke Humphrey this defect in the equipment of both teachers and taught must have come home very strongly, and his reply to the appeal, which was made in April 1438, was not tardy. Already his name, together with those of his father and brothers, was written on that tablet in the Oxford Library which recorded the benefactors of that institution, and in 1435 he had presented both money and books to the University, for which he had received the warmest thanks, and a promise of renewed diligence in study, as recognition that it was his wisdom that had brought about a revival of learning in Oxford. In answer to the direct appeal he had received in 1438, he forwarded what must have been an important part of his library, in the shape of one hundred and twenty-nine volumes, "a more splendid donation than any prince or king had given since the foundation of the University," valued as it was at more than £1000. The letter of thanks spoke in naturally high terms of the Duke's wisdom and learning, and compared him to Julius Caesar, who founded a library in Rome, for he, like Gloucester, combined the attributes of a great soldier with those of an enthusiastic scholar. Not content with their own thanks, these grateful scholars wrote to Parliament, urging its members to thank the Duke, since both they and their relatives had been, or in the future would be, beholden to the University for their education—a request which, it is hardly a surprise to find, went unheeded. On November 5, 1439, an indenture in receipt of the books was drawn up, and thereon were inscribed the first word or words occurring on the second folio of each volume, so that identification in case of loss might be possible. This last precaution, which was customary in most libraries of that period, is still of immense value in verifying the authenticity of manuscripts said to have formed part of the donations of Duke Humphrey to Oxford. Two more gifts followed in 1441, the first consisting of seven, the second of nine books, of which we have only the names of the latter preserved. It is noticeable that on both these occasions the books were conveyed to Oxford by Sir John Kirkby, a soldier who had served under Humphrey in the campaign of 1417. Finally, in 1444, came a gift of one hundred and thirty-four volumes, which were indented for in the usual manner.

Gifts of books in such numbers were unique in the history of the University, and continued to be so for some time to come. Other donors there were, amongst whom may be numbered Bedford, Wheathampsted, the Duchess of Suffolk, Thomas Knolles, and John Somersett. These, however, were all either small collections or single books, and even a gift by Henry VI to the foundation of All Souls only numbered twenty-three volumes. Throughout, Duke Humphrey had led the way in the patronage of the University. He had befriended it at a time when it sadly needed support, and he now endowed it with a library, which in numbers compared very favourably with any similar collection in England. It was a deed of open-handed generosity, which well deserved all the thanks it provoked, for in all he must have given quite three hundred volumes to the University —by no means an insignificant collection of books when all had to be copied by hand. They were drawn undoubtedly from his own private library, as there had been no time between the request and the donations to collect for the purpose, and the gift becomes thereby all the more interesting to us, and all the more honourable to the donor. Humphrey cared not for books merely for the sake of collecting them; he valued their teaching, and did his utmost to give them every opportunity of spreading their gospel abroad among the students of the land.

Special arrangements were made by the University for the preservation of these additions to their Library. Already since 1412 there had been a Librarian, who cared for the books collected in the room over the porch of St. Mary's Church. He was in receipt of a salary of one hundred shillings per annum, besides six shillings and eightpence for every university Mass that he said, and the right to receive robes from every beneficed graduate at the time of his graduation. Only graduates and members of the religious orders who had studied philosophy for eight years were given access to the Library, though certain exceptions, as in the case of sons of members of Parliament, might be made. Oaths must be taken by all readers not to mutilate the books by erasures or blots, an ordinance, let us hope, which was observed more carefully at that time than it is now in modern libraries. The Library was open from nine to eleven and from one to four o'clock, except on Sundays and certain specified days, including the Librarian's holiday of one month in the long vacation.

Fresh provisions were drawn up in 1439 in view of the recent additions. All books were to be entered on a list kept in the Library, and their titles were to be clearly marked on the first page with a list of the contents; none were to be alienated or removed from the Library, save for the purpose of rebinding, though the Duke might borrow any volume after having submitted a written request to that effect. The books were to be kept in chests for the use of lecturers and masters, and in the absence of lectures students might have access to them. In case of loss the loser was to pay to the University the sum marked on the book, which was to be in excess of its real value.

The possession of a useful library did much to restore the old position of the University. From having almost no books—so wrote the authorities to Gloucester—they now had plenty, so that both the Greek and Latin tongue was there studied—that is, both the Greek and Latin authors, for no Greek books were included in the gift. Men from all lands came to study in Oxford now, as they had done before, and the letter concludes with a phrase couched in more intimate terms than had been hitherto customary; "we wish you could see the students bending over your books in their greediness and thirst for knowledge." So great were the crowds that used these volumes, that the accommodation afforded by the old library was insufficient, and so the University wrote to Gloucester, suggesting that the new Divinity school, then in course of construction, should be used for the purpose. It was in every way suitable for a library, being retired and quiet, and the idea that this new home for his books should be called by his name was submitted to the donor thereof for his approbation. Herein we may see a polite hint that money as well as books would be acceptable. We have no evidence that the Duke responded to this appeal at the moment, and he died before the building was completed by the munificence of Thomas Kempe, Bishop of London, who gave one thousand marks for the purpose. With a conveniently short memory the University alluded to the finished Library as *tuam novam librariam* when writing to Kempe in 1487.

This last request of Oxford, though only suggested, did not go unanswered, for Humphrey appeared in the House of Congregation, and publicly promised to give the rest of his Latin books to the University together with £100 towards the new Divinity school, a promise which he renewed just before his death. But this promise was never fulfilled, and in spite of numerous letters to the King, the executors of the Duke's will and many other influential persons, neither the books nor the money ever found their way to Oxford. Even as the library bequeathed by Petrarch to Venice in the preceding century never reached its destination, so did Oxford never benefit by the last promise of her friend and patron.

France

The impulse to collect manuscripts of classical works, which began in Italy in the fourteenth century, spread in the fifteenth to France, England, and Germany. Since many of the old cathedral and monastic libraries were destroyed in the Hundred Years War, our knowledge of

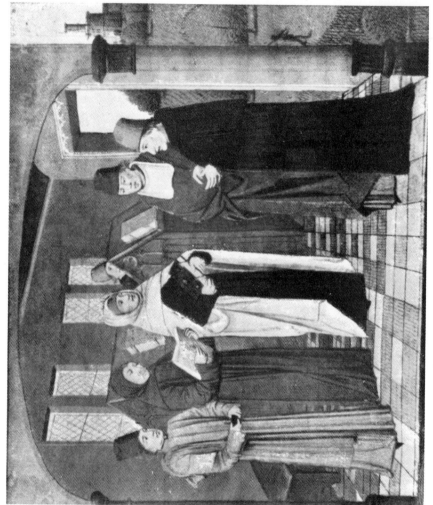

Plate VIII An Early Renaissance French Library

French libraries in the fifteenth century is confined to collections formed by French and Flemish nobles. There were many such collections, including the royal library which was to become the nucleus of the present Bibliothèque Nationale. The appointment by Francis I of the leading humanist of the day to the post of royal librarian is described by Arthur Tilley in The Literature of the French Renaissance, vol. 1 (Cambridge: University Press, 1904), pp. 14–16 and 18–19:

> The leading humanist of the reign was Guillaume Budé. On the very eve of it, in 1514, he had published his first important treatise De Asse et partibus ejus. The popularity which it enjoyed, passing as it did through ten editions within twenty years, testifies to the widely spreading interest in everything that related to the ancient world. Budé was born in 1467, a year after his friend and rival Erasmus. His father was a rich man and had, for the time, a good library; he was, says his son, librorum emacissimus. Guillaume's early education was of a perfunctory character. He was a student in arts at Paris, and in law at Orleans, but in neither branch of study did he reap any profit. It was not till he had reached the age of twenty-four that he was seized with a passion for learning which never afterwards deserted him. The remainder of his life was dedicated to untiring industry, and it was a current story that even on his wedding-day he worked for three hours. In 1520 he published a collection of his letters, including several Greek ones, which definitely established his reputation as a Greek scholar. From this time he was recognized as sharing with Erasmus the primacy of European scholarship. In 1529 he gave a more convincing proof of his powers by the publication of his Commentarii linguae graecae, a species of Greek lexicon which Erasmus had once or twice urged him to write; and which like all his writings is a mass of erudition put together without any attempt at method. Though now of little value its appearance was a notable event in the history of French scholarship.
>
> In the dedicatory letter to the king Budé reminds him in very plain language of the promise he had long before made, to establish a royal college for the study of ancient languages. The project, which is said to have emanated from Francis himself, but

Plate IX Budé Presenting a Book to Francis I

which at any rate was suggested by the college for the study of the three languages founded by Jérôme Busleiden in 1515 at Louvain, had been formed as early as 1517, and one of the reasons for desiring to attract Erasmus to France was the wish that he might take some part in the direction of the new college. But before the scheme was sufficiently matured to be put into execution Francis's attention was diverted by the war with Charles V; and it was not till after the Treaty of Cambrai that weary of unsuccessful warfare he again turned his attention to the arts of peace. The moment chosen by Budé for his appeal was therefore an opportune one, and it was in part successful. Though the idea of building a college and endowing it with revenues for the maintenance of a large body of scholars was for the time abandoned, royal professorships were founded, and on the 24th of March, 1530, the new professors, four in number, entered on their duties. They were François Vatable and Agatho Guidacerio for Hebrew, Pierre Danès and Jacques Toussain, both pupils of Budé, for Greek, and Oronce Finé for Mathematics. Their annual stipend was 200 crowns. . . .

In 1522 Budé had been appointed to the newly-created office of "master of the king's library" at Fontainebleau, and not long afterwards the king began to form there a collection of Greek manuscripts. His first acquisition was made in 1529; it consisted of fifty volumes purchased for him by Girolamo Fondulo, a native of Cremona and a man of considerable learning. In 1542 he bought the collection of Georges de Selve, and in 1545 Cardinal d'Armagnac presented him with twenty-four volumes. The chief hunting-ground for Greek manuscripts at this time was Venice, and here the copying of manuscripts formed a regular industry among the exiled Greeks. About 1540 the most renowned of these copyists, Angelo Vergecio, was persuaded to enter the French king's service.

In 1544 Francis moved to Fontainebleau the library at Blois which he had inherited from his predecessor Louis XII. It contained 1891 volumes, including about forty manuscripts which Janus Lascaris had brought to France in 1508. The great majority of these volumes consisted of manuscripts, there being only 109 printed volumes. In 1545 Vergecio made a list of the Greek manuscripts, which amounted to about 190. In a library like this which had a quasi-public character manuscripts were of more service to learning at this stage of its development than printed books, for they were freely lent to various Paris publishers, and books were thus rapidly multiplied. Before 1528 hardly any Greek books were printed in France, but in that year a real start was made, and four Greek books, all of some importance, were printed. In 1530 the work received an impulse from an unexpected quarter, for no less than eleven Greek books were printed in that year by Gerardus Morrhius in the Sorbonne itself. One of them was a Greek-Latin lexicon. Still greater encouragement came from the appointment of a king's printer for Greek in 1539. The first holder of the post, Conrad Neóbar, died a year after his appointment, and he was succeeded in 1540 by the well-known Robert Estienne, who already held the office of king's printer for Hebrew and Latin.

In August of the same year Budé died, four years after Erasmus. The following words of Calvin give a just estimate of his services to his country. *Gulielmus Budaemus primum rei literariae decus et columen, cuius beneficio palmam eruditionis hodie sibi vindicat nostra Gallia!* The first place in the world of scholarship had in fact passed from Italy to France, and it was mainly the work of Budé.

Hungary

Many other important libraries were established in the fifteenth century. Mention is made of a few of these (including the one in the Vatican) in Géza Schütz's sketch of the famous library of a fifteenth century Hungarian king, Matthias Corvinus. The complete article, entitled "Bibliotheca Corvina," will be found in The Library Quarterly 4 (1934): 552–563 (reprinted with permission of the present holder of the copyright):

The fifteenth century was an age of the acquisition of literary treasures and the foundation of great libraries. During the hundred years between 1365 and 1465, when the art of printing was being established, the birth of several great European libraries took place. The founding of the Library of Paris, the Library of Vienna, the Laurentian Library at Florence, and the Vatican Library in Rome falls in this period. Besides the beginnings of famous libraries, this century witnessed the building-up of the splendid private collections of Charles V of France, of Frederick, Duke of Urbino, and finally of Matthias Corvinus, king of Hungary. The collection of King Matthias eclipsed all other private collections and was considered one of the marvels of the time. The brilliant execution of each manuscript is yet proverbial. Today, about five hundred years after their execution, to possess a Corvina is a triumph even to collectors rich in treasures.

In 1453, Pope Nicholas V founded the Vatican Library from precious freights of classic literature salvaged before and after the fall of Constantinople. As a young man, Pope Nicholas used to say to his friends: "If I were rich I should indulge in two extravagances: in building and in the collection of books." Years later, as pope, Nicholas satisfied both of his early desires. He practically rebuilt Rome during his pontificate. Nor did he neglect his natural inclination for literary treasures. First, he grouped the scattered manuscripts in the Vatican. But he desired a larger and more valuable collection. Book agents were dispatched to seek rare manuscripts in seemingly unlikely places. From dark monasteries, he gathered the works of the writers of antiquity. In a surprisingly short time, he changed the atmosphere of the Vatican bookshelves. During a reign of eight years, the repository of papal bulls became a library of approximately two thousand volumes. The Fathers of the Church—Plato, Aristotle, Ptolemy, Homer, Strabo, Xenophon, and Herodotus [!]— were represented in his library. It was an era of prosperity, the papal coffers were filled, and the pope did not have to consider prices. For a fine copy of the Gospel of Matthew in Hebrew he paid five thousand gold florins. He delighted in magnificently bound copies. His favorites were in crimson velvet—very fashionable at that time—with silver clasps.

Pope Nicholas was not only a collector: he was an accomplished librarian. Whenever, among the literati, the subject of the classification of manuscripts in a library was discussed, his opinion was received as that of an expert. He actually worked out a detailed plan for the arrangement of what he considered an ideal library. This plan was applied in the library of Cosimo de' Medici, and was later copied by other libraries.

Everyone, however, did not pay in order to acquire. Cosimo de' Medici and Poggio Bracciolini ransacked cities and monasteries for manuscripts. Matthias Corvinus, king of Hungary, employed all of the methods at the disposal of a collector and tyrant. When converted to the Italian Renaissance, through his marriage to Beatrice of Aragon, daughter of Ferrante, king of Naples, Matthias felt the need for a great library in Buda. There were a few manuscripts in the palace, mostly from the time of the Angevin dynasty, but these were out of style and in poor condition. However, they served to form the nucleus of the future library. King Matthias was well aware that two high ecclesiastics, Bishop Vitéz and his nephew, Bishop Janus Pannonius, were great collectors of illuminated manuscripts. He, therefore, invited both of them to hand over their collections. The bishops protested. Janus Pannonius pointed out that there were other ways open to collectors. "Italy," he wrote, "is flooded with manuscripts for sale. Send money to Florence and Vespasiano da Bisticci will be able to purvey all of your orders." As Matthias had at first asked for Latin manuscripts, the bishop remarked satirically that, thanks to the courts' ignorance of Greek, part of his collection, at least, might be spared. And, if Greek ever should become fashionable in Buda, he would begin collecting Hebrew manuscripts.

Janus Pannonius actually possessed a remarkable collection. He had bought his manuscripts piece by piece during his sojourns in Italy and treasured them as a true book-lover. This, however, did not stop Matthias in the execution of his project. The letters of the bishops, uncle and nephew, show that the major part of their collection became royal property, *manu militari*. More valuable copies of other Hungarian nobles followed the same route. When there were no more books left to be acquired gratis, the king finally decided to buy them. . . .

Several Florentine artists were engaged in work for King Matthias: Attavante degli Attavanti, friend of Leonardo da Vinci; Giovanni Boccardi, called Boccardino Vecchio, whose first-known work dates from the year 1486; the brothers del Flora, Gherardo and Monte, whose work bears the influence of Ghirlandajo and Botticelli; finally, Francesco d'Antonio del Cherico. . . .

In spite of the steady work of the Florentines, the king's collection grew slowly. To rival other princely amateurs, Matthias invited to Buda a host of Italian miniaturists, writers, copyists, and binders. As their work advanced, a new problem arose: that of the shelving and the proper care of books. Matthias decided to build a sumptuous library connected with the royal palace. Built of red marble, it was situated near the chapel. On its wall was written:

MATHIAS PRINCEPS INVICTVS
INGENII VOLVPTATI OPVS HOC
CONDITIT GENEROSVM

The library was named Bibliotheca Corvina, and each manuscript or printed book that belonged to King Matthias' collection is known as a "Corvina." The library itself was divided into two spacious rooms. One was reserved for Latin, the other for Greek and oriental manuscripts. The light was softened by the multi-colored stained glass of which the windows were made. Graceful columns divided each room into sections. The precious manuscripts, bound in leather, scarlet silk, or crimson velvet, were laid upon artistically carved wooden shelves. . . .

All the manuscripts were decorated with the coat-of-arms of Matthias, showing a black raven holding a gold ring in his beak. . . .

King Matthias confided the direction of his library first to Galeotto Marzio from Narni in the province of Umbria, who was recommended to him by Bishop Janus Pannonius. Persecuted by the inquisition on account of his book, De Incognitis vulgo, he came to Hungary and entered in the services of Matthias. . . .

Another of Matthias' librarians was Taddeo Ugoleto from Parma, who served also as tutor of John Corvinus, Matthias' illegitimate son. Ugoleto made several trips to Florence, the book-market of the fifteenth century, to round out the collection of the king of Hungary. It was probably through him that in 1475 Matthias purchased the library of the Manfredini family of Bologna. With these books, he increased sensibly the number and the luster of his collection.

Little by little, through confiscation, buying, and copying, the Bibliotheca Corvina became one of the most reputed of Europe. It was especially rich in Latin, Greek, and oriental manuscripts. There were very few printed books in the collection, and not one in the Hungarian language. Matthias' collection was remarkable not only for variety of authors and subjects but also for artistic execution and philological value. It is extremely difficult to give a fair estimate of the number of volumes. It was estimated by different authors to have been from five hundred to three thousand volumes. Concerning fifteenth-century libraries, we know that the famous Giovanni Aurispa possessed three hundred Greek codexes; in 1455, the Vatican Library contained 824 Latin and 414 Greek manuscripts. Pius II added 40 to the Greek collection, and later Pope Sixtus IV found pride in counting one thousand Greek codexes. In 1485, the Vatican Library contained 3,650 volumes. Cardinal Bessarion, the great book-lover, had 264 Latin manuscripts in 1468. The catalog of the Este family of Ferrara shows, in 1436, 279 Latin, French, and Italian volumes with one Greek and one German manuscript. In 1495, the same library possessed 512 volumes. Considering these figures, I think that the Bibliotheca Corvina, which was considered the largest of its kind, probably attained about one thousand various manuscripts, estimated conservatively, a figure based also on consideration of the still-existing Corvinas. . . .

Matthias' precious library had the same fate as the empire he ruled. After his death in 1490 it fell into decay. In Italy they feared that now that the king of Hungary was dead, there would be abundance in copyists. In fact, unemployment was provoked there by the manufacture and the sale of printed books. The

Hungarian diet proclaimed that the royal collection would be maintained for the ornament of the kingdom. Notwithstanding the decree, it was ravaged by all those who entered, and the folios served to ornament less princely collections. . . .

The year 1526 was fatal in the history of Hungary. The disaster of Mohács was followed by the occupation of the kingdom by the Turks. The manuscripts that still remained in Buda fell into the hands of the invaders and were removed to Constantinople. Only ordinary volumes were left in the palace. . . . Before the sixteenth century was over, copies of King Matthias' collection were to be found everywhere in Europe except Buda. From this period on, each manuscript has a history of its own. They were silent witnesses of wars, revolutions, treachery, theft, and murder. The mystery that surrounds them, their peregrinations from castle to castle, from damp cellars to dark attics, put a special pride in (and price on) their possession.

Postscript

The books brought together in libraries between the seventh century B.C. and the fifteenth century A.D. were made individually; thus, if a work was long, the task of the copyist was extremely demanding. Books made by hand were beyond the means of most would-be purchasers, so manuscript libraries could be maintained only by institutions with wealth, such as the Church, or by wealthy individuals of the royal and merchant classes. These early libraries were the first organized and sophisticated attempts by man to preserve and transmit his religion, culture, and ideas. As such, they are landmarks in the history of civilization.

When the process of printing from movable types was invented, in the middle of the fifteenth century, the transmission of culture to succeeding generations ceased to depend on the preservation of handwritten copies of a work. Today, manuscript books are made only to commemorate an occasion or to serve as an exercise in penmanship. The comparatively low cost of manufacturing numerous copies of a work has given rise to the distribution of theological tracts, political pamphlets, newspapers, learned journals, business and governmental reports, and other forms of documents which were seldom published in earlier times.

The size of our literate population and the number and extent of volumes accumulated in our modern libraries would have over-whelmed the learned curators of the great library at Alexandria, the largest in the ancient world. But the growth and development of books and libraries as we know them now was dependent on, and be-gan with, the individually-wrought manuscript books and manuscript collections of civilizations long gone.

Index